Conscious

Toxicity

Daria Hsu

Dedication

TO MY PRECIOUS FAMILY: MICHAEL, ZEN AND GAIA. MY GRATITUDE FOR YOU AND TO YOU CANNOT BE PUT INTO WORDS. I AM UTTERLY IN LOVE, AND EVERY MOMENT I GET TO SPEND WITH YOU IS A BLESSING.

Introduction

This collection of poems spans the period from summer 2020 through summer 2023, thus describing three years of our lives. Three years may not seem like a long time, but a lot certainly happened in our family during these years.

The initial setting for my poems is Prague, Czech Republic, where Michael, less-than-year old Zen and I moved in summer 2020 to escape the increasing COVID restrictions in California and, most importantly for me, to move out of my parents'-in-law house and finally start an independent life as a young family on a budget who couldn't afford to live in Southern California on our own. (You can read more about what preceded our move out of California and our early days being new parents to Zen in my first published collection of poems, The Haunted House, also available on Amazon.)

As I learned soon after our move, escaping California and my parents'-in-law house - although bringing us incredible adventures, memories of which will last me a lifetime - did not mean escaping into a life without difficulties. Living in the Czech Republic with my husband and son, I was forced to face severe trauma that I carry within myself: that of being discriminated during my childhood in Prague due to my Russian heritage. In addition, while we were living in Prague in 2020, I continued to suffer from severe emotional and mental torment that was simply unrelenting in the weeks and months since our dear son Zen's birth in September 2019. While in the Czech Republic, I was also faced with the difficult decision whether to meet my parents and to introduce our firstborn to them. The reason this decision was so very difficult was due to the history of a very codependent, painful and emotionally abusive relationship between my parents and me. As a cherry on top, my relationship with my husband Michael continued to be volatile and fraught with many disagreements (as had been the case from the beginning of us knowing each other, but with the added layer of navigating the stresses of parenthood). Because of all of this, staying in the Czech Republic was entertaining for us from the traveling perspective, but it was also tormenting, and I couldn't wait to move to Taiwan to start fresh

Conscious Toxicity
Daria Hsu

without my unpleasant childhood memories following me around everywhere I went.

Our move to Taiwan in late 2020 was an exhilarating and refreshing escape from what seemed too familiar and too painful for me to face. However, despite my fascination with this gorgeous island and its culture and despite our incredible travel adventures all across Taiwan, over time, I was confronted by the all too familiar and highly unpleasant feeling of being an outsider in a country whose cultural norms and language were completely foreign to me. Needless to say, my marriage with Michael continued to suffer painful upheavals in Taiwan. Also, months into our stay in Taiwan, we got caught up in the most draconic-style COVID lockdown we could have ever imagined, which soured our travel experience and basically nullified one of our reasons for moving there, which was to escape strict COVID regulations.

Growing increasingly desperate from our isolation during the lockdown, we decided that we needed to move again. After briefly considering a move to Russia but soon learning that Russia was introducing extremely strict pandemic measures as well, we decided to scrape down our savings and

Conscious Toxicity
Daria Hsu

buy a house in Southern California (Big Bear being the only place we could afford). That way, we would be able to return to the United States, which we came to realize was much more liveable than Taiwan during COVID, but with the guarantee that we wouldn't need to move back in with my parents-in-law, which I was strongly against. After a short stay in the Czech Republic in summer 2021 (short but nerve-wracking because we were unsure if there would be another lockdown and if borders would close, thus potentially preventing our return to the US), we finally moved to Big Bear, California, just before Zen's second birthday, after having spent over a year living in the Czech Republic and in Taiwan.

    Our life in Big Bear was a pleasant one thanks to our lovely, airy home with a backyard, yet the loneliness of living in a very remote location with difficult winter weather as well as my and Michael's often volatile married life caused our family hardships even at such a high altitude. While living in Big Bear, we learned the wonderful, joyful news that our family would be welcoming our second child, lovely sweet daughter Gaia.

Conscious Toxicity
Daria Hsu

In anticipation of Gaia's birth, we decided to move out of our Big Bear home down the mountain so as to live close to grocery stores, playgrounds, museums and other facilities necessary for a family raising little children. We moved into our current rental apartment in Long Beach after brief stays in Redlands and Temecula in summer and fall 2022 (while I was heavily pregnant and we were navigating our living situation) and after welcoming our lovely sweetheart Gaia into this world in October 2022.

I plunged into a deep state of mental/emotional anguish in the months after Gaiapie's birth just like I had in the months after Zenny's birth. Michael's emotional and mental health arguably suffered too in light of extreme stress of us navigating our new life with a toddler and a newborn. Some of the later poems in this cycle describe in a very raw, honest way the severe struggles that both our marriage and my emotional and mental health have faced in the postpartum period since sweet Gaia's birth. However, since all poems in this book were written in the span of three years during which always at least one of our children was a newborn/baby/toddler, the whole cycle could be interpreted from the postpartum

Conscious Toxicity
Daria Hsu

experience standpoint: the emotional/mental, physical-health-related, financial and, of course, marital challenges that accompany the joy of welcoming the most precious little humans into this world.

What became increasingly clear to me as I was rereading my poems is that both I, Michael and our marriage repeatedly suffer from the same recurring problems throughout the years. Situations and locations change, but our issues remain. To finally become aware of that has felt comforting and liberating on some level. A good example of this cyclical nature of the issues we face is my recurring fear of ending up abandoned and alone, either through my husband dying tragically or leaving me or divorcing. Ironically, life has a way of forcing us to face our deepest fears. Thus, one of the poems in this book describes a hit-and-run incident, which happened when Gaia was about six or eight month old and Zen was three years old, during which a scumbag driver hit our car on a residential street in Malibu, almost running Michael over (who was taking Zen out of the carseat at that moment) and immediately escaping in a cruel and cowardly fashion. Another poem in this cycle describes Michael moving out of

Conscious Toxicity
Daria Hsu

our current home in Long Beach (for one night) after our incessant arguing and the devastation I felt during the hours that he was gone.

My modest hope is that although there may be no immediate resolution to our conflicts and challenges, there possibly exists some faint form of a linear, forward-facing trajectory in our otherwise cyclical existence. I am not quite sure what would be at the end of such a trajectory, but I imagine it could be a deeper understanding of our lived experiences, a deeper connection with each other and, ultimately, peace.

May God continue to watch over and protect our family and yours, dear reader.

Daria Hsu

Long Beach, California
August 31, 2023

1.

I'm angry! Fucking angry!
Black, decaying rot is permeating through the thick white mattress
As I throw myself onto the bed, unable to contain my explosion,
With the awareness that I am breaking our son's childhood
Just the way mine was broken
I want him to have a perfect, happy childhood!
Instead, he wakes up to us arguing over a trifle
And me urging you to go take care of him with an angry push

I fail to contain myself enough to go take care of him myself
My world is crumbling
He takes up so much time in my mind:
Yet I'm busy with everything but him
My structured world is shattered, and I fail to provide
Any sense of structure for him while desperately fighting
To hang on to any last bit of control I used to have

Conscious Toxicity
Daria Hsu

I jump back up from the white soft mattress in
angry tears,
Screaming internally, "I hate this! I hate this!"
I try to live perfection,
But instead, what I live is complete and utter
brokenness
My anger has no reason, no containment,
No end, and no beginning
My anger is a black, rotting, destructive mass
hanging above me,
Slowly sinking through my body into the mattress

~

Sinking in a perversely slow, invasive, calm, and
self-assured way
As I convulse in powerless rage

2.

Where is my synagogue,
My community, my people?
They were burned down!
In the fiercest fires of human madness
That only humans are capable of
They burned them down,

Conscious Toxicity
Daria Hsu

And even their souls

So here I am, stumbling through the ruins,
Searching for anything that may have remained:
Maybe a scorched glove? A bloody hand
protruding
From the ruins? Anything to grab onto and remind
me
Of my community, my home, my language:
Because I lost them all

3.

I'm tired of my exile
I want a place that I can call my home:
Where I grew up, belong,
Which I miss dearly when I'm gone,
Which makes me rejoice in sweet relief when I
return
I want a place whose only sin is but a playful
bickering of lovers:
Irritation with each other has subsided,
The bickering becomes lightheartedly
Accepted with a playful pout
Without the bickering, it would not be a home

Conscious Toxicity
Daria Hsu

What am I doing here?
Being the chameleon that I was raised to be,
But not being me
Who am I, anyway, but an experiment of an unjust world?
An outwardly successful one,
But no one suspects the cost of suppressing the
soul's urges for a home taken away too soon

Sitting between two chairs,
Neither here nor there,
All I know is: At the tender age of twelve or maybe thirteen,
In a remote field somewhere in Kaliningrad,
Surrounded by endless wheat, I stood,
And for a brief moment, I felt my home,
My sweet, lost home

4.

I want to be included, to belong:
It pains me deeply to hear your language
That I do not understand, your visible enjoyment
Of connecting while feeling like a fifth wheel

Conscious Toxicity
Daria Hsu

You are so close with them...
So, do you belong with them?
That leaves me by myself, without belonging
If I turn on my chameleon and try
To learn your language and blend in,
Will I give up the remainder of myself?

It's a difficult choice:
To act, pretend, be submissive to your culture
And be rewarded with a fake semblance of
belonging
While being haunted with never-ceasing
reminders
That I'm a newcomer all along -
Or to refuse any attempts at assimilation
And choose to feel excluded and alone
Ironically, the wound of fearing that I don't belong
Can be traced back to my origins -
I don't feel like I belong where I came from

5.

I make sure to give you
Lovely pecks on the cheek
And brief kisses

Conscious Toxicity
Daria Hsu

As reminders of our love
And yet our love, I feel,
Died at the moment his life started
He did nothing wrong
Unless being a lively rambunctious
Awesome baby is a sin
But why do I feel like my life ended
When his just started?
The heaviness, lack of excitement,
Constant anxiety, what ifs,
We're doomed, I'm cursed!
Constant need to perform in order not to drown
Is my new normal
Unlikely in the past,
Yet routine now, killing me slowly,
Like this new, perfect family life

6.

I want to accomplish so much
I have so many dreams for me, for us
But our lives are finite
How to sustain infinite dreams,
Dreamy expectations of boundless opportunities,

Conscious Toxicity
Daria Hsu

Exciting pathways opening up in front of us in all directions,
With seemingly endless, fun, surprising detours to suit our every wish and whim,
When our bodies have an expiration date,
When all dreams - even if achieved and lived -
Must end, be covered in flowers, then be buried -
Hopefully with accolades -
Then graciously give way to others' dreams,
Which, in return, one day,
Must also be buried and give way?

7.

I am afraid to look into your eyes
Because, should I do so,
You'll punish me
You stand there in the distance,
Big and buff,
Your eyes fixed on me every second,
Drilling holes into my heart
My arms, my neck, my back are filled with tension,
My head consumed with how to act natural and non-suspicious
When you suspect my reason to exist

Conscious Toxicity
Daria Hsu

As you approach me,
My terror grows
I am completely, fully at your mercy,
Of which you only have a drop,
Only just enough to keep your human designation
Not enough to let me live, just to exist
I am an oxygen robbing animal to you,
A worthless bug that you despise
Should I look directly into your eyes,
I'll lose the very last of life that you've allowed me
to keep,
My bare existence, my oxygen, my food
That I eat half-cooked as you kick me randomly at
will
With your black mighty boots,
I'm huddled over my plate,
Hoping to take up as little space as possible,
So you notice me less, bruise me less frequently,
Hoping I will magically disappear
Becoming invisible to you
Will end my suffering,
Yet I'm still here and by cruel irony of fate,
I'm doing everything I can
To prolong this miserly existence[1]

Conscious Toxicity
Daria Hsu

[1] This poem is about my experience with a xenophobic waiter at a Prague restaurant I visited with Michael and Zen. I grew up in post-Communist Prague (Czech Republic) and, as a child, was heavily discriminated due to my Russian heritage. This has left a painful lasting imprint on me.

8.

Relax? Do nothing for a while?
I am not sure what you mean
I am a perpetual motion machine
My brain is on and never stops
Enjoyment is not part of my vocabulary
Enjoying the big and little blessings of life,
Baby, sex, family, surroundings, good health, strong body,
Sounds good in theory but how
When I'm afraid to stop?
Because if I stop,
I am afraid to fall back into the haunted house that I escaped,
That I escaped to only end up in gray, busybody normalcy

Conscious Toxicity
Daria Hsu

9.

Almighty God,
Would you come into my heart and save my soul?
Would you come into my bedroom and save my marriage?
Would you heal my body?
Would you bring forgiveness into all facets of my life?
Would you teach me not to fear hardship,
Not to be bitter about giving of myself to others,
And to know that I will lose none of myself as I do?
Would you grant me peace to take time to sit back,
Meditate, contemplate,
To get out of the eternal cycle of struggle,
movement, pain, worry, anxiety,
To feel the joy of my beautiful soul more often?
Would you help me heal my wounds?
Thank you, God

10.

All I ever wanted was to know that you are fine
That my people, long forgotten,

Conscious Toxicity
Daria Hsu

Beaten, famished, misrepresented, kicked,
Have silently triumphed
In a non-show-off, quiet, content way
That my people had forgiven and moved on
From hurts and egos
That somewhere in tree-rich country,
They were growing again,
That they had quietly won -
Without openly battling,
Without attacking those that had tried to eradicate
~
After living in sweat and pain for generations,
In God's sweet kingdom,
That they had suffered much
But had gained faith throughout,
That we may all be stranded at one point
But remain tied together in our pure hearts,
resilience and faith
That's all I ever wanted

11.

The pain in my arms is the pain of sore, exhausted
muscles,
Holding onto one's own child's lifeless body,

Conscious Toxicity
Daria Hsu

Muscles that so reliably, so loyally would strain to comfort him
In the warm cradle by one's own heart
As he was drinking milk and dozing off into sweet baby sleep
Are now being strained just one last time
Before his little, sweet, fragrant little body
Disappears forever under the ground
Despair that cannot be expressed in words nor comprehended,
Just like the logic of a psychopath,
Two, three generations later, I feel it:
In my arms

Is God a psychopath to have allowed it so to happen
That a mother had to bury her only, little son?
Diseases, accidents make possibly sense
When we have been around for a while,
But when it comes to angels sent to us from heaven,
One cannot help but wonder if madness in this world
Is but a reflection of madness in the sky

As I sit here many decades later,

Conscious Toxicity
Daria Hsu

My heavy, healthy boy with tiny sniffles and just the teeniest bit of fever
Is sleeping comfortably in my arms
While suckling for sustenance, health and endless love
I am within a three-minute walk from the local hospital
And close to a century removed,
Yet his warmer than usual body,
His sniffles, his few coughs have thrown me off decades back,
My arms aching with what perversely
So many have gone through yet so few have spoken of,
My mind is temporarily lost to reality
As in concealed terror, I'm trying to prepare
In a most efficient manner for his approaching death,
Internally punishing myself for choices that I'd made,
Ready to lash out at my husband for choices he had talked me into
Too late. He's headed towards death to join my uncle
Whose name I don't remember, whose grave I'll never see

Conscious Toxicity
Daria Hsu

His unusual warmth, his little wail sends me into
the same hysteria
That my grandmother probably felt at her little
son's cold body

12.

We were not nurtured ourselves,
And yet we're asked to nurture
To open our hearts, caress,
Take care with patience, hugs and reassurance,
To do our best for others
While we ourselves feel so malnourished
On the love we have received:
Conditional, unwilling, strained
Maybe, if we were to understand
That we were born into uncertain times,
Times of upheaval, sudden and scary change,
To parents who themselves were wounded
And malnourished on love
From their own wounded and malnourished
parents,
We could forgive and start again
A new life that we're so wary of starting,

Conscious Toxicity
Daria Hsu

But this time around, appreciate every piece of
peace,
Every slice of bread, every ounce of freedom that
we have,
Give our children the rainbow fragrance of peace,
love,
Joy, faith, healing, honesty and growth
That were denied to us,
That we have no more excuse to deny to them
When we forgive, learn and move past,
Empowered by our divine victorious light,
New life will grow in us, from us,
And divine light will help our mother Earth
Illuminate brightly our infinite universe

13.

Have you ever wondered what it's like
To return to the place of your own rape?
To walk in constant terror of running into IT
Somewhere, anywhere,
The thought of your eyes meeting -
Just for a moment, in a perfectly safe public place -
Causing you to break out in cold sweat
Because you know that once they meet,

Conscious Toxicity
Daria Hsu

IT will be laughing mercilessly, cruelly
Right into your life-drained eyes,
At the death sentence IT pronounced upon your soul
The day IT penetrated you against your will?

Or maybe IT will stare at you sadly, with a lonely sigh,
Demanding more (as if there were more to give),
Whining, reproaching,
Or maybe, as you accidentally catch a glimpse of IT,
ITS back or profile,
From a far corner of a public space,
You will feel electrocuted despite IT not even noticing you,
Not paying you the slightest attention,
Your whole day completely ruined
By the downward spiral descent into the abyss
On whose precipice you have been so carefully, courageously balancing
Have you ever felt what it is like to walk this Earth
In terror of turning around each corner?

14.

Conscious Toxicity
Daria Hsu

I guess I left my heart somewhere mid-way
On a windy, sunny path through
My home's fields -
Fertile, rich, naturally part of me, I part of them,
Like leaves are part of trees,
And embryo part of a mother's womb -
Where no one asked me where I'm from,
Or where I'm headed,
You wouldn't ask that of a tree,
But simply enjoy its peaceful presence
And then in gratitude you'd let it be

I walked so frivolously along that path,
So naturally part of the whole,
It never would even occur to me
That anything other than basking in gentle sunshine,
Walking my path in peace and harmony could possibly exist
But through forces that remain to be explained,
Clouds stormed in, unpredictable storms clouded my life,
And, already battered, I was torn from my loving, sunny field,
Humiliated, beaten up, then cast aside

Conscious Toxicity
Daria Hsu

Such untold stories of flowers are many, many...
Rise up and tell:
You shall be heard

15.

When all you've known is pain,
Then maybe, maybe you could look past
The grayish face, the sinewy, bluish hands
When you've never felt loved,
Then maybe, possibly you could forgive
The forehead permanently wrinkled up
In tense, uneasy concentration
If you had never received mercy,
Then possibly, you'd comprehend
The almost insurmountable task
Of reaching out to others with arms full of mercy
If you have cried yourself to sleep in darkness,
terror all alone,
Then maybe, maybe not, you'd come to understand
How faithlessness, brutality become some people's
native language[1]

[1] This poem is dedicated to my mother.

Conscious Toxicity
Daria Hsu

16.

We're fucking poor,
And that's the way we live
We painfully count every penny as we argue
Over what we can do without
We're fucking broken,
And that's the way we live
In silent anger, ready to explode,
We don't see our ripped clothes,
But others' holes stick in our memory too well
We feel a mix of fear and mercy for them,
But little do we know that
We are them, and they are us

We juggle every penny,
Sometimes there are many
Sometimes they sound like rain in distant
Amazonia,
And we feel overjoyed and happy
As we bathe in newfound faith fueled by plenty
We juggle left and right, and up and down
We juggle on one leg, cross-legged,

Conscious Toxicity
Daria Hsu

While jumping in midair, while standing on one hand,
And take increasing pride in being so majestically skilled

But then the circus ends, and pennies disappear
Into seeming nothingness like the Amazonian rain did
We sink into confused despair,
Angrily rip our clown's wigs off our heads,
Puzzled by what went wrong,
Faith gone

17.

Marilyn!
I know exactly how you felt in that Spanish house,
No furniture in the bedroom because
Your mind was everywhere, just not at home,
Your soul aching in pain,
Your mother on whom you gave up
Still in your heart
I gave up on her as well
Your dark, black bedroom blinds

Conscious Toxicity
Daria Hsu

Unyielding to the California sunshine attempting
to come in from outside
I remember them from my own mother's house
I am so scared of them

My mother lying on my childhood couch,
Pale like a corpse,
Barely able to lift her hand or pronounce words,
Signing to me to make the room even darker
Me trying to extinguish her pulsing head on fire
With a hurriedly patched together cold towel
compress,
Sometimes helping her get up
So she can vomit in the toilet - a scary sound!
But also a ray of hope
Because bringing a bowl for her to vomit on the
couch instead
Would surely have meant that she was near death

Me calling the ambulance in barely contained
terror,
Their number, address itched in my memory like
my own name,
The whole process rehearsed too many times
before:
Picking up my mother's wallet from her bag,

Conscious Toxicity
Daria Hsu

With shaking hands finding her insurance card
While waiting for the adults' arrival,
Uniformed men picking up my mother's barely
living, barely walking corpse,
Taking the bus alone to follow her to the hospital
emergency room,
And - hours later after lonely, jittery anticipation
in the waiting room -
A ray of hope as my beloved, only mother,
Weak, pale, slow, but able to walk unassisted and
speak,
Appears from behind the emergency room door -
Her lease on life renewed with IV painkillers that
can't be prescribed,
My faith, however, still tarnished with dark blinds
I struggle to open

18.

I'm cold
It's freezing here
But it's not so much the wind outside
As it is these old, gray plastered walls
Missing wallpaper, revealing ages old newspaper
scraps

Conscious Toxicity
Daria Hsu

That emanate the lack of warmth,
Broken children's hearts,
Shaky, ever-changing minds,
Cruelly destroyed faith,
Survival motions on auto-pilot,
Everything beautiful and worth living for
Frozen into an icy kingdom under eternally
overcast gray skies
With ever unnerving, dribbling, inhospitable rain,
Able to melt children's hearts in adult bodies,
Which are so sweetly dreaming of blooming
In the majestic, light-filled spring's arrival,
But which are also wary of spring being
interrupted once again,
Inevitably turning into an icy kingdom yet again,
Too scarred to survive another blow of fate,
Yet imagining many
In short, these walls are full of mourning that
never was
Of tears uncried,
Of screams turned inward
Because the safe space to take a break
And openly mourn was never there

I imagine myself on a train somewhere in Siberia,

Conscious Toxicity
Daria Hsu

Passing by never-ending, snow-clad, sleepy spruce trees,
Not a smell of a human nearby,
Mesmerized by this monotonous majestic scenery
That knows and understands more than I shall ever do,
Finally finding the tranquility needed to mourn and to find peace
Somewhere here, they murdered my great-grandfather
Like a hunter shoots a rabbit, no second thought
Somewhere here, my orphaned teenage grandmother
Dragged her freezing feet from house to house
And begged for food from strangers in order to survive
Somewhere here, she lost her firstborn,
Only baby son to meningitis
These tall, majestic trees have seen it all
They know it all, they keep their secrets well,
And somewhere near the Urals, they took my other grandfather
And threw him into jail to rot for decades
Mercilessly,
Because there is no other way to steal a father from his wife and kids

Conscious Toxicity
Daria Hsu

The blood and tears that seep through earth,
The screams of horror and despair that walls
absorb,
Where do they disappear?
They never disappear
I see and hear them

19.

On this cold, gray day,
When nothing is happening,
And it feels like nothing will ever happen for
another thousand years,
The nature and the town have come to a complete
standstill
I am sitting with my feet pressed up against the
warmth of our kitchen radiator,
Consumed by a health scare and hopelessness
triggered by a slightly crampy stomach
A nervous, painful boredom forces me to feel the
pain I've been escaping
With planning, playdates, the usual daily business,
the trips across the Czech Republic

Conscious Toxicity
Daria Hsu

I'm staring out the window at the many lives in front of me in the apartments across from us,
Attempting to imagine what they're like
Their windows are dark behind blinds and curtains
Such intimate proximity to mysterious strangers that I'll never meet,
Or will meet but won't recognize
Rarely, an occasional gray head pops out of a window to have a smoke and meditate on the state of our street that has not changed for decades,
Or to look with elderly suspicious mistrust at this new scary world from the comfort of its top, seventh floor apartment
Are we all hiding behind windows, waiting for something to happen, or is it just me?
Another cold, gray fall with these cold, gray neighbors and an occasional wheezing of a tram passing by in the distance,
The ultimate quiet, but not a peaceful one for m
This grayness was subdued in summer,
But the monotony of the day-to-day grind is catching up,
The clock of time mercilessly ticking, summer inevitably had to end

Conscious Toxicity
Daria Hsu

How to survive this gray, cold, dead stillness that'll
last for months,
In which nothing ever happens, no friendly shouts,
no joyful faces, no street celebrations,
When I am sleepy, achy, mildly irritated,
dissatisfied, in pain behind this window,
Grasping for the little warmth of the kitchen
radiator,
Trying not to freeze on the outside and on the
inside?
How to find some light, and peace, and joy
In this perfectly proportionate, gray, icy kingdom?

20.

Son!
You'll meet my parents
They've caused me pain,
They've made me cry, still do
My mother told me that if your dad and I ever
have a child,
She would refuse to hold them in her arms
My father told me that your dad and I would not
last
In short, they have been nasty to me,

Conscious Toxicity
Daria Hsu

They still are
But nastiness is often the outside layer of deep pain
and fear
My mother's father refused to hold her in his arms
after she was born
My father's mother did not want him and my
mother to last
My parents, unknowingly, perpetuate the pain, the
nastiness of previous generations,
Unloading it on me my whole life
I ask myself, why even make an effort to meet
these people
Who cause me nothing but heartbreak every single
time?

Rather than live your whole life in confusion,
wondering who they were,
And how that relates to who you are and what you
go through,
Rather than run away from immense pain and
trauma of many generations,
Ingrained in their DNA beyond repair,
You have the right to meet and see them for who
they are,
To witness brokenness and sweetness, tears and
pain

Conscious Toxicity
Daria Hsu

And - hopefully - at least a little bit of light, a little bit of mercy,
But don't count on finding those two within them,
Cultivate both within yourself

No less important, although I see the nastiness in them,
I almost always fail to recognize it in myself,
And so I, your own mother, perpetuate the hellish cycle
Into our own family with you and dad
I call out my parents, I cry over my parents hurting me,
And yet I tend to cause similar pain to you and dad,
And as I do, I'm mostly blind just like my father and mother
I'm lost in pain and fear like they are
I end up nasty like them
In short, this isn't a warm cake and coffee relaxed kind of family get-together
We're about to have
It's one of many buried traumas and possibly outright hostility and toxic ways,
But just remember, Zen: things are the way they are

Conscious Toxicity
Daria Hsu

They are not bad or good
They're there for us to witness:
To witness the cycle of pain perpetuated in our family
From generation to generation,
And to walk our life's path beautifully from here

21.

This may be a sob story, but I take responsibility:
I gave myself to you completely, fully, with my heart – again
Oh, me, the fool! What was I thinking?!
I left my mother's poisoned choke hold
Only to find myself in yours, years later, in the noble name of love...
No matter how much I gave,
There was no applause coming,
No mercy, no soft caress
I got entangled more and more
Into your chilling web spun from exclusive ownership, vengeful manipulation
Yours is a one man's land, and I am but an ant in this pained kingdom

Conscious Toxicity
Daria Hsu

Your trauma rests royally - behind a fancy, foggy veil - on a laurelled pedestal,
While mine was tossed aside, sacrificed in the name of nothing,
Inconsequential to your world except for being a convenient pillar for your captivating theories of light and healing
Your pain is an excuse for every way you hurt me in our home
My pain is an inconvenience to you, a burden on our family: "Why haven't you healed it yet?!" is your reproach
Your pain manipulates me into guilt, self-doubt each single time
Your pain is buried carefully and deeply from the world's eyes,
Displayed by you in a controlled manner, in controlled doses onto the world,
And yet at home you slam it mindlessly, mercilessly, without awareness onto your closest loved ones
Heal yourself!
I want to see you grow from here
This is no way to build a family with me

Conscious Toxicity
Daria Hsu

22.

Dearest mother,
You will forever be the reminder of brokenness to me,
That this world is so plenty with
The email alert from you -
That seemingly tiny, innocent beep-beep from my Inbox folder -
Will forever cut like a dagger through my heart,
Raising my heart-rate in nervous suspense and
Terrorized anticipation of what's to come
I am simply afraid of you
I know not to trust you,
Anything I say will be taken with a grain of salt
I am the grain of salt in your eyes.
Your natural dislike of me,
You being unnaturally fed up with me,
Repulsed by me,
Yet always on my back and never wanting to let me go:
What kind of sick love is it?
A manipulative, tainted, painful one
I searched for that kind of love,
I am ashamed to admit,
In all the wrong places:

Conscious Toxicity
Daria Hsu

Insecure, sleazy men I couldn't trust,
And a teenage girl, broken and bent just like me
You are a statue, mother,
To the neighbors' daughter who cries so
Plentifully, deeply, without consolation, every day
And gets beat up for it
You are a statue to the neighbor
Who almost bangs a hole through our
Red gate in her uncontrolled rage
Because her unfulfilled heart
Prevents her from enjoying uplifting,
Joyful baby music in our front yard
I will forever rethink my every word with you
Because I know instinctively, proven so many times before,
That it will be misunderstood,
Serve as yet another reason to repulse, trigger, anger you,
Be used against me in a heartbreaking, undermining way
I shall, therefore, forever censor myself
From saying all I truly wish I could say to you,
To the warm, inviting, loving mother in my mind's eye,
Into whose arms I would so love to sink,
For whose warm embrace I yearn

Conscious Toxicity
Daria Hsu

With all my body, all my soul
That warm cocoon of mother's warmth,
Her body heat, her love, her plentiful milk, her beating heart,
It is the paradise on Earth
I cannot have that mother in you ~
But I can become that mother myself
May the all-powerful, all-wise universe
That deprived me of that
Nurturing, all-accepting, calm milky warmth in you
Assist me in radiating this energy from within myself
Amen

23.

Sweetheart, I am so grateful
For you giving me this life,
For living this life with me,
For our lovely, lovely child,
Another one to come, patience, grasshopper
What we are living is so uniquely beautiful
It's not just wake-work-eat-duty-play-sleep
No, it's heaven on Earth,

Conscious Toxicity
Daria Hsu

Every moment is our souls' bliss on Earth
Challenges are meant to come up,
You know it well, my love
We chose them back in heaven
To learn to feel closer, love deeper,
Grow in our beautiful commitment
My darling, we can do it
Despite feeling at times that
Days are hard and nights are even harder
We can keep our destined soulmate love, our bond
While having given a happy childhood
To our gorgeous, precious children,
A childhood filled with love.
The heavens are cheering us on!

24.

Darling,
Why is it so hard
To simply enjoy all that we have?
Why does an all-consuming cloud of darkness
Follow me around to the most fun places?
Why are baby duties that are meant
To be enjoyed and cherished
Being performed on auto-pilot,

Conscious Toxicity
Daria Hsu

With a half-absent, tortured soul and mind?

I guess that nothing really changed:
You're still the same -
I'm still the same
However, now, we're burdened
With a responsibility for another life
Without having fully figured out our own
We're fighting hard not to inflict wounds onto Zen
While often drowning in our own wounds

Every day, life unravels in front of our eyes
In all its magnificence and hardship,
And I so wish I'd learn to take it in,
Truly enjoy our days with our sweetest, precious bug;
I so wish to lie down by your side at night,
Beloved,
Our bodies intertwined, like they used to
Seemingly a thousand years ago,
In hugs, words, giggles, cuddles, jokes, caresses,
With heart-melting lightheartedness and innocence
That seem to have escaped us,
Embodied now in Zen

Conscious Toxicity
Daria Hsu

25.

Why did I not treasure you when you were with me?
Why was I so lost in my depression, darkness, pain,
Forever lost in things that are not real
But seem so overwhelming and so infinite?
Just for a split second, when I called your name into the street
And heard no answer back, I thought I lost you!
I lost you to my pain
I chose my pain, my wounds
Over your love, over joy, over your sweet faces,
Your laughter, hugs, caresses, kisses,
And for a split second, as I stood there in darkness
In horror, I realized what a huge and irreversible mistake
I had been making, choosing my sadness, drowning myself in it
While joy was within arm's reach
It was right there!
In front of me, behind me,
Hugging me every day of my life, every minute of my day

Conscious Toxicity
Daria Hsu

What excuse do I have to say no to it?
What excuse do I have to say no to love and happiness?

26.

I am a broken woman,
A woman who is in pain,
A woman physically abandoned by her father at birth,
Emotionally abandoned by her mother,
A woman often not present with my son the way he needs me to be,
A woman lost in ocean-deep fear, pain, traumatized numbness, shame,
Excessive worry, complete disassociation from the present moment like generations of women before me,
A woman absolutely terrified of birthing another woman,
Terrified of birthing a daughter for fear of not loving her,
Not nourishing her, not being there for her, losing her,

Conscious Toxicity
Daria Hsu

For fear of perpetuating what often feels like an ancestral curse on the feminine
What can I do with all this pain?
There must be something I can do with all this pain that is too heavy
To carry on one slim, hunched, thirty-year-old back:

Wounded women wound children and men
So women, fight hard to heal your wounds,
And men, don't wound your women
Women's toil is silent yet it moves mountains
Their toil bears, nourishes, protects, raises future generations
Without many accolades in public or in private
Women make the world go around
Yet often hear ridicule, contempt for mentioning
Even a semblance of this age-old wisdom
Women belong in positions of power,
Women's voices deserve to be heard and respected too
Women, it is time for you to begin to listen -
Not to the anger or the thirst of revenge within you

~

But to the generations-old wisdom

Conscious Toxicity
Daria Hsu

That lies within each and every one of you, your psyche, your body,
Your female instinct, simply by virtue of being a woman,
To begin to appreciate your femininity in all of its magic power:
Your unmatched strength, your body, your feminine energy, your ancestry, your wounds
Feel them, explore them, speak them, heal them
In healthy, vibrant womanhood lies the strength not only of all women, but of all men on Earth

27.

I am deeply wounded
I am not whole
My femininity is wounded
My nurturing, mothering side is broken
I bring with me the broken femininity of past generations
I'm uncomfortable with my inner world
I am uncomfortable with my emotions
I am afraid to stand up to my partner in fear of being abandoned

Conscious Toxicity
Daria Hsu

I carry the terror of being emotionally abandoned by my mother
And physically abandoned by my father,
Of being emotionally manipulated and abandoned by my angered mother every time I dared to stand up, speak up, say no
The terror of her response to my no has taught me to not say no
My parents knew no better, I am told
My soul chose to be born into their family
I am learning that a mother, although incredibly important, is not the whole universe
I have angels and spirit guides swirling around me at all time, pointing out the way to me, protecting me
If I had not had them in my childhood, I would not have survived it
Which proves that parents - being incredibly important - are not the whole world the way I used to think they were
What am I doing? My parents were too lost in their own childhood pain and thus unable to be present with me as a child
I am too lost in my own childhood pain and trauma and not able to be present with my own child!

Conscious Toxicity
Daria Hsu

I would love to connect with my mother over our
shared experiences of womanhood, motherhood,
our childhood experiences
Instead: I can't even look her in the eye with
understanding
We're mother and daughter, we're women from
the same tribe,
Yet due to unhealed pain and trauma and
miscommunication,
We're aliens from different universes to each other

28.

Every day is a struggle
I fight my husband and his demons
I fight to give a happy childhood to our son ~
The one I did not have
I struggle with my own soul's demons
I fight to make money for my family,
To have food and luxury
I fight to keep my marriage intact
And my family at peace
Amidst explosions, discouraging news
And headaches from silent crying

Conscious Toxicity
Daria Hsu

But the ironic thing is that -
Unlike in a battle -
I do not have the option to surrender
I climb into the shower, half-choking on tears
I hide from our son for fear of traumatizing him,
And from my husband because of my pride and
ego after he was - I feel - an ass to me
(I must be an ass too, I just don't notice in all this
insanity)

Finally warm, hot water pouring onto my
exhausted soul and body
Finally, something to myself... A shower... Alone, in
peace,
And I tell myself:
"If only I can survive today, that's all I need
I can't control my husband's choices,
His soul, our son's soul, each person has their own
Lessons to be learned
How can I simply concentrate on being
A decent mother, a decent wife, a decent human
being,
On learning - without constant fear and fretting -
my own soul's lessons?"

Conscious Toxicity
Daria Hsu

29.

Mother,
I think I judged you way too harshly
It doesn't mean what you did, how you were didn't hurt
It means: Now, I understand
As I am standing in the kitchen, my head
Heavy like a kettle with an undiagnosed mental illness
(Remember? You used to say that:
"My head is heavy like a kettle"),
I am torn between cooking lunch for my family
To sustain some sort of normalcy for us
And poorly attempting to keep at bay
A simply indescribable, all consuming, about-to-rage
Terror attack while glimpsing with my inner eye
Into the hopeless, darkest pit from which
I fear I'll never climb out if only I give in to this panic attack
But I have the most loving, present, caring husband
To take care of our beloved son while I have a chance
To give in to it in privacy, to break down in peace,

Conscious Toxicity
Daria Hsu

Away from our child's eyes and ears,
Ultimately fighting to glimpse peace and heal

But how did you do it, mother,
With husband gone, you and me alone?
I take my hat off to you for all that you did do
I always reproach you for having failed here and there
I - as your child - have major, dark wounds
From spending my childhood with you
I - as a mother - suffer mental, emotional anguish
And sometimes I simply pray to make it through the day
But judge you I shall not
I now am standing at the precipice of the same dark
And hopeless, lonely pit at which you have been standing
For at least as long as I have known you
The emotional, mental anguish feels
Unavoidable, destructive, paralyzing, isolating
But I am so blessed in ways that you were not
Surrounded by pure love, determination in my heart
You and women before have lit the path,

Conscious Toxicity
Daria Hsu

It's up to me to shine on it brightly and unapologetically
So that the whole world can see
What all of you, mothers, have heroically -
In silence, pain, despite all odds - accomplished

30.

I'm playing with our son
We play baby music instruments and sing to Christmas songs
We build factories and skyscrapers out of Legos
I'm so glad I get to spend this time with Zen,
Having fun and teaching him
Michael is coaching clients in the bedroom for one hour,
His door is closed for clients' privacy and to keep out the noise
As one hour passes, and then another fifteen, twenty minutes,
I open his calendar to double check when his session ends
It was supposed to end twenty minutes ago.
I did not see him go inside the room before his session started

Conscious Toxicity
Daria Hsu

I was too busy taking care of Zen
So, I start doubting myself: Is he really in that room?
I continue playing with Zen but in my mind the image comes:
After waiting another thirty minutes, an hour without him coming out,
I finally open the door and find an empty chair, an empty table,
No one in the room
I open the door and look directly at horror, nightmare, devastation, irreparable heartbreak,
My husband gone without a trace
As my fourteen-month-old son is standing behind me and innocently demanding to play more,
This image unsettles the previous calmness in my chest, tightens my throat
I keep playing with Zen but am no longer present with him
I ask myself: Did Michael have a heart attack? I go into the kitchen to drink some water
And tell myself: The longer you wait to check up on him,
The less chance he has to survive
I go toward his door, knock lightly so as not to disturb his client session,

Conscious Toxicity
Daria Hsu

Barely open the door and look through the crack:
Michael is sitting in front of his computer, two
people on his screen
I immediately shut the door,
Relieved, but not really
The downward spiral has been set off:
My shoulders and arms heavy with growing pain
and anguish,
The mind racing and now bringing up further
issues from earlier today
They had seemed almost trivial but what I just
experienced now is an understandable reason for
my heavy kettle of a head
And depressed chest heavy with hopelessness, lack
of interest, joy,
Slowly accumulating tears behind my eyes
I need to withdraw from my family and find
something to soak up my full attention:
Coloring, playing piano, observing construction
through the bedroom window,
Watching sunset over crushing ocean waves in my
mind
In the last few days, I noticed that it appears to
break the chain
Of the unfolding, growing tornado inside my
mind,

Conscious Toxicity
Daria Hsu

Helps me reset my mind back to calm and peace

31.

I erect a monument to all the present fathers:
To my husband,
To his father who taught him by example,
For staying
While the wife is going through emotional anguish, mental torment, unimaginable hell with no end in sight
As she is trying to parent their child with numerous blunders
But to the best of her abilities given her seemingly all-consuming pain
That clouds her lovely soul struggling to navigate the tasks of this Earth
I erect a monument to the fathers who quietly,
Without awards and accolades,
Day after day,
Night after night,
Year after year,
Lovingly step in, care for their child,
Care for their wife at her lowest of the low,
Rinse out her bowl of vomit when she's sick,

Conscious Toxicity
Daria Hsu

Patiently feed little bits of chicken to the young
toddler for what seems like hours,
Lie by their wife's side in bed and comfort her with
loving hugs,
Wash dishes, change diapers
Without complaining, without reproaching,
Without heading for the door,
Without impatiently asking, "Are you better yet?"
Instead, they tell their wife,
"Rest and sleep while I take Zen out for a walk"
They are overwhelmed themselves with something
bigger than they had ever bargained for,
Yet they stay on, love on
With patience, compassion,
And at times (probably more often than I will ever
know)
With silent sacrifice
Fathers who are present,
Your names are eternally etched in Heaven
My husband,
My beloved,
Your healing love has grown into my fragile
Yet, thanks to you, increasingly blooming heart
For an eternity

Conscious Toxicity
Daria Hsu

32.

As I walk around our house saging,
Zen in tow,
I sing:
I am not a child of trauma,
I am not a child of trauma,
I am not a child of trauma,
I am not a child of trauma,
I am not a child of trauma
I am a child of bravery and perseverance,
I am a child of daring courage, love, and humble hard work,
I am a child of foresight and forgiveness,
I am a child of never losing faith,
I am a child of deeper understanding
But I am not a child of trauma,
No, I am not a child of trauma

33.

We try to live and we survive,
But do we really thrive?
You'll find no carefree smiles on our faces

Conscious Toxicity
Daria Hsu

Instead, they're wrinkled with constant worry,
fear,
As if the trauma of previous generations were
happening to us,
As if war, poverty, and human madness were just
about to destroy our family,
As if all faith was futile in the face of an
approaching disaster -
That's how we live,
We, faithless bastards, children of trauma

We truly have it all: but we're not happier
Than have-nots
Under our roof there isn't more peace than under
others' roofs
Despite their own hardships and pain,
Our parents have given us their love and care to
the best of their abilities
While surviving under demons of their own
Our child's eye doesn't see the sacrifices of
immigration,
The terror of a life in the eternal shadow of war
and revolution,
The unpredictability of an unstable country
It sees a mother fraught with pain, terror,
depression, fear,

Conscious Toxicity
Daria Hsu

A mother who does not thrive, radiate, glow in darkness,
And with our every frown, raised voice, and doubt
We perpetuate the cycle into Zen's childhood,
Into future generations,
Perversely toiling so hard to give and sustain his life
Only to destroy, numb, injure it with our failure
To thrive vibrantly,
To radiate light unapologetically,
To find courage,
To breathe life

Oh Zen, how I want to live and breathe life!
My lungs are starved for life!
Before we die, we must learn to live, my son!
To simply live

34.

Last night I had a dream:
We're sitting in a stadium
They're sitting on the upper level, some of them with guns,
And we're sitting on the lower level, right below

Conscious Toxicity
Daria Hsu

There's tension and such anger
The upper ones and lower ones are fed up with
each other,
Furiously yelling and trying to prove to each other
why the other ones are wrong
Everyone feels disrespected, unloved by those from
the other level
Eventually I'm so fed up, I begin yelling at the top
of my lungs:
"All of you need to calm down!
Don't you realize what you are doing?
This is civil war right here!
Of course, we must respect every human being
I can't believe I have to tell you all this!"
Some people (from both levels) nod in agreement
as they listen up
I proceed to talk about my family and our half-
Chinese, half-Russian baby son,
The wonder and the beauty of love across borders
Which we ourselves have rigidly created
But soon, the stadium grows impatient
People begin rising from their seats,
Ready to leave,
While I persist and continue yelling at the crowd
I will not give up on my message,

Conscious Toxicity
Daria Hsu

But my voice is dying down among the increasing restlessness
So I get up, ready to leave as well
There's nothing left for me to do here
I walk out onto the stairs, ready to go down and leave,
Suddenly, a rumor begins circulating that downstairs, there are people with guns
We decide to try going down a different staircase,
But as we are about to descend someone comes running up,
Informing us that there is a gunman under that staircase as well
We can't leave, we've been taken hostage!
The most terrifying thing,
We can't escape through windows either
Because the gunmen have positioned themselves on the third or fourth levels
From so high up, it would be a certain jump to our death
We don't even know how many of them are policing the outside premises
So, I climb up the stairs
I remember in my dream that I used to live on the top floor,

Conscious Toxicity
Daria Hsu

And I know that there still are bed sheets stored there
You see, a similar darkness happened in Russia[1]
when I was a child (feels like a hundred years ago),
So I have an idea for an escape route from a hostage situation:
We shall build ropes out of bed sheets and at night,
When the gunmen are hopefully unable to see the outside clearly,
We shall escape,
We shall climb out through windows and down on ropes into freedom
Then we'll run away fast before they have time to target and shoot us

[1] 2002 Nord-Ost siege in Moscow

35.

I feel so depressed, so hopeless, so lonely,
And it would be easy to blame it on the world I live in
Yes, the world I live in is far from the world I had envisioned

Conscious Toxicity
Daria Hsu

Myself living in, I saw (still see, still hope, how much of it is a delusion?)
Us living in a beautiful spacious house in California,
With a panoramic swimming pool, not too far from the ocean
So that we can drive there on weekends (and weekdays, if we please),
But as I get myself into the details of this vision, the many soulful friendships,
The casual, friendly California banter at Trader Joe's,
I catch myself realizing I barely had any soulful friendships in California,
And the banter that I used to enjoy disappeared with lightning speed in March or April 2020
Taiwan is no exception to the realities of life,
But it feels exciting and new here, although also challenging and foreign, with the added complexity
Of a language I don't understand (or make any attempts to learn)

The new COVID regime adds a new layer of complexity to what was already brewing underneath the surface:

Conscious Toxicity
Daria Hsu

My and other humans' emotional pain
There is no denying that something is missing from this world:
I can't quite put my finger on it yet,
But I believe to have caught glimpses of it here, in Taiwan
However, before I delve deeper into what's missing in humanity,
I need to answer what's missing in me?
Why did I wake up feeling a longing for connection?
I'm feeling lost without soulful ties,
I'm feeling faithless (yet acting like everything is fine)
I need to find my faith…

36.

Hey honey,
I wanted to buy a single-family house in Frisco
I hear everyone is moving there
Nice and big,
New construction,
Or maybe built in nineteen-nineties?

Conscious Toxicity
Daria Hsu

We could rent it out, with an option for us to live there some day,
And let's get another house somewhere in Dallas, maybe Houston,
Since everyone's moving there and prices are soaring
I'd hate to miss out on the profit;
Investing makes me feel so good

Hey honey,
I also wanted to buy a third house in California
I'm not sure where since we're already buying two in Texas,
All cash of course,
But I'm thinking Sacramento? Central California?
Southern, Northern... There are so many options
Laguna Beach, if we are really lucky
We've made a lot but lost even more,
So we don't have the money quite yet,
But if I toss and turn our investments just enough,
Maybe take out a loan or two,
We could make it work

Yet somehow today for the first time,
I don't feel the strong desire to join that endless race for profit, for more cash,

Conscious Toxicity
Daria Hsu

I'm starting to feel more at peace with staying
behind while seemingly everyone buys houses in
areas with skyrocketing prices
It would be lovely, don't get me wrong
Growing our investments feels nice,
But don't we have enough already?
There were times, honey, we couldn't pay for rent,
And look at us now, we pay rent and buy toys for
our son, food, drinks galore
We live by breathtaking nature, a river, rolling
never-ending hills of green, over which sun shines
so beautifully and which on rainy days are
adorned so mysteriously by fog
Without participating in that never-ending
struggle for more, without the Joneses, we realize
we have enough, exactly what we need and want -
not more, not less
And with our souls belonging to us, not to profit
and corporations, we're lucky
Sweetheart, we're so lucky!

37.

Grandmother Maria,
Grandpa Ivan,

Conscious Toxicity
Daria Hsu

Grandparents Alexandra and Vladimir,
Both my uncles,
All my great-grandparents,
My cousins and my niece,
All my relatives, living and diseased,
I will find you
I'll excavate you from the ground with my bare hands
I don't mind, I'm not put off by gravedigger's dirty work,
For it is a mere child's dig into a sandbox
compared to your hauntings I inherited and constantly relive
I'll dig you out,
Pry open your unwilling mouths,
Untie your tied tongues,
I'll finally get the answers:
What, when, where, and above: why?
The never-ending sorrow spanning generations,
I need to watch the replay of all that transpired back at least a hundred years
To finally be liberated and understand.
Give me that DVD, that YouTube account, that Amazon Prime subscription,
So I can watch and analyze from a safe distance,

Conscious Toxicity
Daria Hsu

For I can barely handle witnessing the after-effects
in my crying elderly mother,
Lost somewhere between genius, profound
wisdom, paranoid hush hush, delusional putting
on of masks, and a little girl's angry, very, very
broken heart,
But I need, I desperately need the answers so
I can enjoy the here and now - just for once -
without being tortured,
So I don't grow old crying just like her

38.

The big elephant in the room is my undiagnosed
bipolar,
Or rather cyclothymia
I'm lying on the couch all day,
Not able to get up, not hungry, shunning all
contact,
Life and sunshine outside,
Relaxing music and Fiji beach footage on TV,
Listening to M (she is such a star!),
Completely overwhelmed,
Weakness in my body,
Pain in my soul,

Conscious Toxicity
Daria Hsu

And the worst guilt about the way I feel, the way I am,
Surrounded by the loveliest creatures of all: joking, kind, patient Michael,
Playful, laughing, running Zen
My guilt telling me,
"Get up, act like nothing's wrong and go out with your family,"
I realize my mother told me,
"Get a hold of yourself"
just a few days ago on the phone when I complained,
But don't I deserve a little bit of kindness,
To linger on the couch,
To cozy up, swim in my feelings rather than try to suppress out of guilt,
Find power in my body's weakness,
Swim on the waves of me, me, me...
The way I am, the way I was created,
My body, soul, sensitivities, and all...
I'm staying put on this couch until I am reborn

39.

I found my San Francisco

Conscious Toxicity
Daria Hsu

I found it on our rooftop in Taipei
I spotted the Marina district so clearly
Among tall palm trees, blue sunny sky, and tall
brown residential complexes
I found my happily forever after
Over sushi and Japanese beer,
As I chanted loudly, "Xinnian kuaile! Xinnian
kuaile!"

I found my California
In the Riverside Park by the Taipei Zoo
My mystical, foggy imperial China I found
On rainy days somewhere along the path of
Maokong gondola
God! So much peace I found when just for once I
dared stay still…

I found my Italian Riviera on the wall tapestry of
our fifth floor apartment
I found Hawaii standing on the Wanshou bridge,
And Fiji on our TV screen
My Staten Island, New Jersey, my nineteen-nineties
Russia I found on Muzha Road, at section four
by the car wash

Conscious Toxicity
Daria Hsu

And on the sixth-floor balcony I felt my soul, my divine soul
I finally learned to live my craved California dream seven thousand miles away
While taking in tall palm trees and never-ending rolling hills of green

40.

Maybe I should be kinder to the way I feel
Instead of blaming, could I learn to love myself,
Even the parts of me which hurt, seem inappropriate and destructive?
Maybe I should give myself a hug,
A warm bear hug for the clumsy, restless, nervous me
That keeps frantically running from one room to another
Trying to accomplish so much while Zen is napping,
Hitting corners, spilling tea while he's awake
Maybe I can learn to give my trauma some gentle loving,
That nervous, anxious anticipation of the worst,

Conscious Toxicity
Daria Hsu

Of Michael disappearing forever every time he
leaves the house
Maybe I can give myself some grace,
And while I do, I'm beginning to hear a new voice
in my head telling me,
"He'll get some fruit and dumplings and return"
Maybe I finally deserve some mercy and
forgiveness
I've given them to others, so why not to myself?

41.

I just want to be happy
I know that I need to stop overthinking,
Stop being in my head so much
I want to connect with my heart,
To find my presence and my peace inside my
heart,
To dissolve in the current moment,
Let go of my headache caused by overthinking,
Let my stagnant, rigid body erupt in a carefree,
wild dance,
And yet I catch myself thinking, worrying
What will remain of me if I decide to let go -
Forever - of my pain?

Conscious Toxicity
Daria Hsu

I catch myself wanting to let go of it,
To feel light, happy, free,
Yet still wanting to keep it as a backup option
somewhere secret, safe inside me,
Like a sadomasochist who appears like your
average content and normal Joe in public
While doing strange, dirty, shameful things in his
house's underground/cellar
I have a mortal fear that I will dissolve if I let go of
my pain inflated, lifesaving ring forever
Forever is a scary word, a decision not be taken
lightly
To walk into light without a chance of return
Is a surprisingly difficult choice

It all boils down to this:
Deep down I am mortally scared that I will lose all
connection, forever, to my mother if I let go of all
that weighs me down
My only connection to her being our shared pain,
our trauma, our headache, our overthinking, our
embittered perception of loneliness
Losing all connection to my mother - not just for
now, not just eighty five percent of it but all, with
no chance of restoring it in this or future lifetimes,
Saying goodbye to her forever,

Conscious Toxicity
Daria Hsu

That amounts to death

And so I wonder:
How can I let go of all my pain and move into a
space of innocent joy and peace,
Appreciating the wonderful life I have been gifted,
Without ending up motherless for an eternity?
How can I keep my mother in my heart
While keeping my heart pure of pain?
My heart has been repeatedly broken into a million
pieces,
Witnessing, hearing, feeling her for thirty years
Deep down I wish to give her one more chance by
baring my soul, my all to her,
In a sincere hope that I may finally connect and
become one with her craved warmth
My inner voice (her voice?) steadily reminds me
that it will be *my* fault if I lose her forever

42.

We live on in our children:
The beautiful and the ugly,
The light and the scary,

Conscious Toxicity
Daria Hsu

My biggest grief, regret, and shame being to hear,
think, realize that I'm not providing a peaceful
home for you
Feeling this failure is
Bigger than my anger at my parents,
Bigger than my heartbreak over my own
childhood,
I spent three decades mourning, suffering,
critiquing my parents,
Only to come to doubt my own parenting after
hearing the reminder from psychic L this morning
to keep a peaceful home for Zen,
That a blowup in our relationship is coming,
This set me off on my usual overthinking,
worrying, depressive spiral

But boy, oh boy! I just want peace!
I want no more war
I want to shove my anger up my anger's ass
Because that's where it belongs
I choose to choose peace this morning
I'll take Zen to get bananas, papayas, AA batteries,
paper cups, and cheese,
And then I'll do my first day of breathe yoga with
Adriene

Conscious Toxicity
Daria Hsu

Just for today, for now, I'm choosing peace and I will walk from here

43.

I can feel your pain, dear K
With my tightly constricted throat, I can hardly read the book to Zen without emotionally breaking down
I am reading cheerfully "Time for a Hug" to him
As I am trying to get his attention back to the pictures of rabbits, trees, and sun,
I myself am not present as I read because inside, I feel seemingly inexplicable panic, anxiety, and sadness
My voice is about to break down
I don't want to break down and scare or scar my toddler,
To cause him to see his mom is cuckoo with her reality-disassociated, spinning head

We are all interconnected and despite my life right here in the now being sweet and wonderful,
Being surrounded by love, in warmth and freedom,
We're all interconnected through space and time,

Conscious Toxicity
Daria Hsu

And so, I honor, dear friend, your pain, the brokenness inside you
It but reflects the brokenness of the whole world
That can, however, be healed, be mended,
If we choose to see and honor the light of the world that is available to us
I often feel distant, irritated, questioning, puzzled, intrigued, critical stares
Which used to make me feel so completely alienated from my surroundings,
But I have been choosing to look these strangers in the face,
Each one individually, and recognize the love in them behind their stares,
For love is everywhere, it surrounds us wherever we go
We only need to choose to see:
Love always existed, it exists, and it will always exist,
Like that kind person on the helpline who talked to you for thirty minutes
That's love! You only need to keep reaching out
I commend you for that because I tend to hide when I'm in a crisis

Conscious Toxicity
Daria Hsu

I feel laughable and unworthy of love or
compassion, ridiculous and cuckoo when my head
and soul spin out of control,
But in reality, we all have demons to acknowledge
and wounds to heal
So, keep reaching out for love, my dear,
For where there's love, there's light!
And you and I are light - even though we are
broken, bruised, underslept, with spinning heads
of anxious worries

44.

In recurring arguments between you and me,
You try to make your voice heard,
To stand up for your deep-seated pain
I try to make my voice heard,
I know I'm right and you're in pain!
And so, we get lost in proving to each other our
pain, our right, our voices
But...
Who will make our son's voice heard when we
argue?
We are so lost in defending ourselves that we
completely fail to defend the most vulnerable
human among us... Our dear child!

Conscious Toxicity
Daria Hsu

And so, the child suffers, unheard, growing up
among adults in pain
Who couldn't care less to protect his voice,
To make him feel worthy,
To consider his point of view,
To make his pain heard,
Because they are too lost to pause
For a moment and consider that they are inflicting
on their beloved child the same pain they live in
themselves

45.

My dearest son,
You gift me some of the most beautiful, precious
moments in my life,
And I thank you for that,
Memories to be cherished forever, tearfully,
tenderheartedly,
Knowing they can only happen here and now,
never to return as I age (oh, I fear old age and the
grayness it haunts me with! I hope I can carry my
free, joyful, dancing, wacko soul through old age
with that Aquarian grace I so take secret pride in -
In other words, I hope I grow old and turn into a

Conscious Toxicity
Daria Hsu

fun, wacko, kind, witch-of-light grandma - a skinny hippie in long, colorful, airy dresses and skirts - joyful, my depression transformed into light, compassion, love and wisdom)
As you are suckling on my left breast and sleeping at ten-o-three am Taipei time,
I momentarily want to reach for the camera to capture this beauty to enjoy when you and I grow older,
But thoughts of a society dumbfounded by the sexualization of a breastfeeding mother and child sour this thought for me
And so, I watch you, teary-eyed, my infant, my baby, my toddler,
As you are gently, sleepily, innocently suckling on my left breast with eyes closed in a pure bliss of comfort and security
This is perfection!
This moment, this view - this is heaven, this is perfect - this is when worries, fears and problems dissipate - they don't exist on this plain
This is love
The only true perfection because this perfection is of God's kingdom, of light, of life's source

Conscious Toxicity
Daria Hsu

Dear son, I and your father are so grateful to be
living by your side, to be witnessing your
childhood, our dearest most precious son
You are blessed by us, our love and faith in you
surround you always

46.

Girls, what you did today,
You honestly broke my heart
It doesn't matter that you're five or six
And I am thirty
As you kept running around me in circles and
mockingly shouting at me in broken classroom
English, "How do you do! How do you do!" while I
was cheering Zenny up and down the slide
Made me feel five again
I felt myself turning into the center of the
playground, I already draw looks by virtue of my
non-Chinese heritage,
But this was so, so, so very painful to be mocked
I felt so powerless,
It reminded me of my childhood when I was a
communist Russian to my Czech surroundings, an
unwanted classroom loner in pain, a ridiculed A

Conscious Toxicity
Daria Hsu

star student, projecting strength and courage while on the inside my heart kept weeping, no one available to protect and hug me as my heart - bless my heart! - was dying from shame and pain
You thoughtless girls, you're growing older and testing your boundaries with adults,
And I must stay adult and can't smack the heck out of you or kick your butt as I wish I could,
Although when you grimaced at Zenny when he innocently reached out for your sparkling purse, you were getting closer to pushing me toward my boiling point
For him, I will kick your butt
But for myself, I will simply weep inside powerlessly and without any support

And you, annoying boy, kept circling around me and Zen and exploding in laughter every time my eighteen-month-old angel tripped and fell on the playground stairs, and kept tapping him with your hand to get a reaction out of him
While Zen - remaining true to his name - gracefully stayed on his playful path, not getting distracted by your sorry shadow

Conscious Toxicity
Daria Hsu

Children, where do you get your bullying meanness from?
I know my son doesn't have it in him
I doubt you were born with it
I suspect your parents' pain, the pain at home, the pain of society, the pain of generations is what you are channeling into your interactions at the playground
Your parents - and I - are savages ourselves
We've simply learned to hide our pain and act it out in private - on our family members, on our beloved children - behind closed doors
The playground is just the tip of the iceberg
And yet love and redemption are possible
Our world desperately needs healing
We, parents, are in desperate need of love!
How can we teach genuine connection, universal love, not just being polite - so that our children enjoy (and share!) playground slides in joy and peace?

47.

What am I doing to myself?

Conscious Toxicity
Daria Hsu

I deny myself sleep by spending half the night on
the phone surfing the Internet mindlessly
I head straight to the ice cream section in every
dining buffet we visit
I can't live a day without milk tea from the corner
tea shop
When something stresses me out, I reach for a few
slices of chocolate to calm myself down,
Deal with health consequences, emotional and
physical, later - don't even bother acknowledging
a possibility of them in the moment
I try to be most loving to my son
But how can I teach him self-love if I regularly
engage in self-hatred?

I am a tormented soul with childhood trauma,
mother issues, father issues, ancestral trauma
But clearly grace has not escaped me
Oh no, God blessed me with the sweetest love of
my soulmate-husband, our lovely son, kind loving
parents-in-law, and dear friends, I lack in nothing
material either
When I am able to see through the dense fog
surrounding me, I see the strongest, brightest
white light surrounding me most lovingly and with
an unwavering dedication

Conscious Toxicity
Daria Hsu

I feel chosen, blessed, and loved
I feel special
The goal of my life is to learn to hear - through my hazy fog - the deep, beautiful truth that the Universe, God, my guardian angels and spirit guides are shouting at me in joyful unison:
"Daria! Live and enjoy!!!"

48.

I can't sleep tonight because I ache from what I witnessed and from the knowledge that my son is growing up surrounded, touched by pain
I saw it in M's bulging, pain-engorged eyes as she was gazing upon me
She may be a mother of two but
Becoming parents ourselves, we don't stop being children,
Still reeling from our parents' divorce,
Every day reliving the shock of a sick mother, non-present mother, a mother not available the way we need her to be,
Still secretly convulsing in a helpless child's pose from craving the warm, unwavering embrace we never got,

Conscious Toxicity
Daria Hsu

Reliving our mother's terror of anxiety, our father's helpless, slighted anger at the unfair, hurtful world he himself witnessed too soon

I cannot sleep tonight
I am rewatching in my mind's eye yesterday's happenings in the playground sandbox:
A menacing finger wag at Zen, an angered, "You shouldn't throw sand!" from the said Russian father, the four-year old's slighted dumping of wet sand in Zen's direction (what started as Zen's playful attempts to catch the older boy's attention in order to play together quickly escalated into war!)
The Taiwanese grandpa's light slap on Zen's fingers for trying to take his grandson's toy car
Some other child supposedly not wanting to play and share with Zen
But I also remember the kindness of a father who patiently dug into the sand with Zen, taking time from his own child
Thank you!
Love and war exist side by side

So, what are we going to do about this pest, the pain?

Conscious Toxicity
Daria Hsu

The only pain we truly can't avoid is death, some
diseases, accidents, and natural disasters
Everything else can be conquered, transformed
from pain into lightness and light by a resolved
human spirit so as to no longer fester
As to the pain that's unavoidable, we need caring,
loyal, warm support networks
We need the brotherhood of man, the sisterhood of
woman to carry us safely through rough oceans

49.

There's so much pain in the world,
And people are so blind, so deaf to it
They have cut off their intuition and choose to go
about their day
There's something so psycho about all of this,
Wetiko

You'd think people will rise up together against
pain, punish the abusers, save the abused
There certainly seems to be a lot of talk about it,
But why then did I witness a beggar crawling on
the dirty market street, worse than a dog, crawling
and kissing the dirt of the earth like a rat?

Conscious Toxicity
Daria Hsu

And tens, hundreds of people around her were going around their usual daily hustle and bustle, not noticing her, passing her by as if she truly were a rat?

After the initial shock, I finally dared to look her in the eye - it was ... unsettling, scary, I awkwardly smiled (or grimaced) and looked away

In my mind's eye, I kneeled by her side and asked her, "How can I help you?"

I knew that thirty Taiwanese dollars Michael gave her at my urging wouldn't save her nor end our world's savagery and psychosis

But in reality, I didn't kneel by her side because I was afraid of people judging me and afraid that she may ask for too much, what if she asks for something I can't give? And thus, I walk on by

Why did I witness a girl sexually abused by a creepy old Taiwanese guy at a playground the other day? How is the world in so much pain that it's being perpetuated into my son's generation?

That's not right

She came to the playground with her "grandfather" and started sliding down the slide like any kid, a little teenage girl

But upon a closer look, it was more like sprawling over the slide - her body possibly a bit too old to be

Conscious Toxicity
Daria Hsu

sliding on a toddler slide but definitely too young
to be climbing all over the old fifty-plus-year-old
man, sitting on his neck, seemingly reaching for
his groin, sitting at the bottom of the slide, her leg
intertwined with his leg, his hand on her thigh
I knew that he knew he was doing something very
wrong at this dark, desolate playground that Zen
and I had ended up at by pure chance, he knew he
was stealing her innocence, her childhood from
her
I became afraid and kept acting like a stupid white
foreigner not suspecting a thing (for once, the
stereotype worked out in my favor) but I was
secretly taking photos, I felt resolute right there
and then to go to the police station and to file a
report
The girl was barely noticing Zen but whenever she
did, it was almost with bitterness, and I knew
exactly why:
Zen has something that this girl has been robbed
of, a childhood
I believe even Zen could sense something was
amiss
Eventually I took him to another well-lit
playground with lots children, to my relief
But that girl, she still haunts me, two days later

Conscious Toxicity
Daria Hsu

I haven't gone to the police
I am being discouraged by Michael
I tried to post in Taipei City Playgroup for feedback
and help but the admin denied my post
I posted on Facebook, Instagram, picture and video
- no comment, silence
I am not going to the police because I don't have
their names nor addresses and in my heart, I sense
that Michael is partially right when he says, what
are the police going to do?
But in my heart, I also know I need to do
something
I can't see a child in pain and move on, sipping my
berry juice and nibbling on nuts and chocolate and
pretending like it didn't happen
Michael is right that we have to change the world
by healing the emotional pain of the world because
that's why beggars are crawling unnoticed on our
streets and young teens are being inappropriately
touched by old men
I am growing in understanding why my parents
were so strict in my teen years
(Too strict! But I can spot their line of reasoning
now)
I can't remain silent
I will go to the police today

Conscious Toxicity
Daria Hsu

Will I go to the police today?
Wetiko.

50.

Oh, my love,
Words could not describe,
There is not enough paper in the world
To fit my praise, love, and gratitude for you,
My sweetheart, my gentle, loyal soulmate,
Loveliest creature of all,
You've given me, you give me a life
I could have only dreamed of
You are the silent hero
You love me the way a woman should be loved

You've patiently climbed up stairs back to me ~ never mind you being in a hurry ~ when I was yelling at you in my powerless rage, lost in my heartbreak, terrified of my inability to complete everyday mothering tasks, lost to your love, lost to our child's wonder, lost to my own mind and heart, in panic
You have honored me in every possible way
You have loved me to the moon and back

Conscious Toxicity
Daria Hsu

My blessed, kindred spirit,
Your sweetness permeates the air
My gemstone,
I love you

51.

I go crazy when you leave me home alone
The freedom of it petrifies me
It is no freedom; it is chains not knowing when
you will return
You left to run some errands,
Hours later, I realize you are gone with no
Certain time of return, with no
Way to contact you, with nobody for me
To alert about my acute, hysterical aloneness
That wholly consumes my brain, my body, my
breath even
With its terrorizing, seeming finality - or infinity,
shall I say?
I wander through our apartment, shell-shocked
By the fact that you are gone and I have
No idea when, if you will return
I open the apartment door into the empty hallway,
Empty stairs, closed doors,

Conscious Toxicity
Daria Hsu

Quiet, no one coming up or down, and certainly
not you
Surprisingly, my terror still has ways of growing
It turns into a panic attack, I shut the door with
shaky hands
I grab the little icon of Jesus -
The only safe object, the only human available to
me in the here and now -
Resigned, I drop into a chair and start talking to
Jesus:
Jesus Christ, please make my mommy come back
home
Please, Jesus Christ, make sure she comes home
healthy and safe
Panic and terror over my complete
Five-? Six-? Seven-year-old isolation at the top of
this empty staircase
Inside the agonizing quiet of our huge, old
apartment
Are slowly giving way to the resigned (almost)
calm of grief
And so, this morning, my love, when you left
To the paper store and then stopped by the print
store across the river,
Taking longer than you promised, I could not sleep

Conscious Toxicity
Daria Hsu

I crawled up in a fetal position on the living room carpet and cried out in silent terror
While beloved, sweet Zen was sleeping in the nearby bedroom,
And then I walked into the bedroom and saw on his precious face
The most beautiful, sweetest smile - he was smiling in his dream -
Oh Zen! You can mend broken hearts with a single smile, my love! -
Zen reminded me, why am I even crying?
Nothing's wrong, everything is quite perfect
Actually, why am I crawling on the floor like a fetus?
As I lay down by his side, I was able to begin to calm down,
But then as my inexplicable grief took hold of me again, and I started quietly crying,
I was surprised to taste the tears of my childhood, that same taste,
That same painful pressure in my stuffy nose
I used to throw myself on the carpet in my childhood room in Prague
And sob in what felt like complete confinement and hopelessness of my living situation with my parents

Conscious Toxicity
Daria Hsu

But amidst this morning's painful reliving of my childhood terrors,
I was startled by the growing question, why do I continue throwing myself onto the floor
If I am now surrounded by the unshakable loyalty and love from my husband
And by the healing sweetness of my one and only son, Zen?
I am increasingly wondering these days,
Was I made mad in my childhood like I used to believe,
Or was I born mad to a mad mother?
Will I give birth to a mad daughter in return?
And if so, what tools can I give her?
How can I support her through this madness?
I have been told something along the lines of focusing
On the here and now (which helps, for sure),
On sleep (true that!),
On leaning towards light (I tend to drown in my depression, ashamed to admit),
But I also don't want to treat this madness like something to be swept under the rug,
To turn away from
I want to get to the bottom of this demon,
After all, it isn't stronger than me

Conscious Toxicity
Daria Hsu

And ~ I'm not going to lie ~
The high of coming out of this funk feels
exhilaratingly good,
But the healthiness of being attached to this
Cycle is questionable

52.

This past night I dreamt of my past college crush,
Extensively, endlessly, tortuously
He is holding a movie screening in his dorm room
He announced it in advance and I ~ so desperately
~ want to come
But we are off, not on
So I crave him in quiet desperation,
Dreaming as I stare through his dorm window,
Infinitely turning left and right in my bed,
Waking up with an achy back
I am a married woman with a child,
But I give myself permission to go ahead and look
up his photos
I study up close his muscular arms,
The shirt tightly stretched over his breast,
One breast seemingly more protruding than the
other

Conscious Toxicity
Daria Hsu

It can't be, it must be the shirt or an unlucky angle
of the camera?
I fixate for a few moments on that visual flaw,
Wanting to pull up that shirt
Then I zoom in on his face,
He has long hair now
Did he have long hair back in college?
I want to say no but I am no longer sure, I can't
remember...
I fixate on those full lips
I kissed them once (or twice?) at night in the
arched college hallway on the way to my dorm
room
I study his face: why my nightlong fascination with
it now?
Why the uneasy, sudden obsession?
Knowing no details from his current life other than
what I can gage from a few photos on his Facebook
profile, I conclude:
He is single, no kids yet, a graduate student
He has not yet been thrust around by life in the
way you are after starting a family
His vagina and anus have not been ripped and
sewn back together
It is unlikely he is dealing with hemorrhoids,

Conscious Toxicity
Daria Hsu

Or wondering when he will find time to take his
vaginal steam bath or apply yeast cream or even
just eat a full breakfast or dinner
My exhausted, breastfeeding, malnourished,
underslept body with no period and no unpaced,
leisurely sex in sight,
With a small hand and a small foot alternately
hitting me in the face and ripping glasses off my
face,
Seems to yearn for some of that individuality he so
unquestionably retains
His dark long hair... I need to wash my hair
His face... I look so beautiful with washed up hair,
even more so without glasses
Yesterday at the indoor playground, I must have
looked like a hot mess compared to N -
She also has a little boy, nine months older than
Zen, yet she manages to wash her hair,
She doesn't wear old, loose, scratched up glasses
That's it, I must set up a resolution:
I will shamelessly claim my time today to wash my
hair, to shave my legs and armpits, to order new
glasses, and to order - for the first time in years -
new contacts
This mama is gonna get spicy!

Conscious Toxicity
Daria Hsu

53.

I yelled at you this morning and raised my voice at
Zen too,
And now I'm regretting it
You took him out to play and eat upon my request,
So I can have time to relax and get a haircut,
And you disappeared, for an hour and a half not
answering my messages on Facebook,
And I am getting increasingly anxious as the kind
hairstylist is patiently caring for my hair and
gently massaging my exhausted, overthinking,
over-worried, under-washed scalp,
Repeatedly telling me how beautiful I am
She is reminding me that in my anxiety there is
abundant love available to me,
That we are all knots of love in a giant net of love
and support with which we have the capacity to
cover the whole Mother Earth
As I enter our empty apartment, still not having
heard back from you, I break down crying,
Looking at the ceiling, hopefully my guardian
angels can hear me as I deeply regret having been
impatient and irritated with you both, my loves,
this morning, before you took off

Conscious Toxicity
Daria Hsu

Hopefully my guardian angels can see the loving heart underneath my unkind thoughts of irritation as Zen was playfully, lovingly attempting to climb onto my back while we were looking up videos of different kinds of birds together...parrot, eagle, pigeon, penguin, chick (not same as cheek, sweet Zen!), flamingo (Zen's favorite)

It's hard to navigate between giving my all to our son and our lovely family, the blessing of Michael and Zen in my life - these most adorable, goofy, loving sunshines in my heart,

And needing much-needed rest and me-time, a recuperation of a relaxing haircut, a warm long shower, an undisturbed lighthearted catch up with an old, dear friend...

But it's the hardest to navigate the regret, the guilt Of having raised my voice and pushed away my loved ones with my angry outburst stemming from overwhelmed exhaustion,

Of not having been the most loving mother and wife,

Of having contributed even the slightest trauma to our child

It is shameful to traumatize our child

It is a heartache that lasts for decades

Conscious Toxicity
Daria Hsu

My heart still breaks and tears are on the verge of
streaming from my eyes when I remember the
shock of my mother breaking down in angry tears
and pushing me away when I was trying to play
doctor with her for probably the hundredth time
while she was lying down to rest
Twenty-five years later, my inner child is crying
and telling her in my head, "Why did you become
angry, cry and push me away? I was simply having
a good time and innocently playing with you! I
was being a child!"
So today I regret that I was silently trying to
prevent Zen from climbing me and that I raised
my voice at him for playfully slapping my face,
reaching for my nostril, and attempting to take off
my glasses
He was having a grand old time and simply being
a child
I had woken up exhausted and in a grumpy mood
I apologize Zen
I apologize Michael, my love, for all those times I
yell and forget I yelled

54.

Conscious Toxicity
Daria Hsu

Help me!
I don't know what is wrong any more,
Nor what exactly I'm escaping or where to escape
My husband is unhappy with where we are
Outside on the street, people have turned into mask-wearing,
Fearful, angry zombies
I don't see an apocalypse or feel it,
But I feel stuck: where do I go from here?
Where do we go?
What's best for our son?
I thought we had escaped the lockdown craze
We were the lucky ones to have left California and Czech Republic for Taiwan
But now Taiwan is introducing new restrictions
There are four levels, we're on level two
With the possibility of going up to level three,
Which is basically a lockdown
They do anything they want to us
Yet people like zombies follow commands
N told me her husband passed out and shook from the vaccine
But her response was, "Imagine if he got the virus!"
She's lost to the fear-mongering,

Conscious Toxicity
Daria Hsu

Messaging me that one person with the virus went
to Costco a few days ago
And that she hopes we didn't go there at the same
time
Like I care!
How can people allow propaganda to completely
brainwash them?
But what hurts more is that my husband is pining
for his parents,
And instead of celebrating our life and all we have
achieved together: independence, family, freedom
(now beginning to be curtailed) - he wants to go
back into the womb
He is not shining his manhood, safety, and security
into our marriage,
Instead wanting to be reunited with his mom and
dad
He is not willing to have another child now -
preferring to postpone
- but why, I ask?
There's nothing to wait for,
Life is in the here and now, and I want to live it in
the here and now – fearlessly
There's enough BS in other people, I don't need it
in my own husband

Conscious Toxicity
Daria Hsu

I want to grow our family - to have one, two, three more kids!
To witness Zen be the most loving brother to his sibling(s) -
How precious, beautiful, and fun for them!
I want to visit Russia - the land I'm from, the mythical land - I want to see it
Especially in today's world that seems upside down...
Is Russia just as bad, I wonder?
Is it more free?
Do people there know the truth?
What is the truth, I wonder?
But I know suffocating myself in 33-degree heat in fresh air in broad daylight ain't the truth
I know that injecting myself with something that causes people to faint and shake while the absolute majority of uninjected people are healthy or recovered just fine ain't the truth
And I know that living in constant danger mode and escape mode ain't the truth either
Neither is refusing to grow, to take the next step, to pause our life the truth, Michael...
We are life partners for a reason:
To have adventures together, to grow together, to explore unexplored corners of Earth together, to be

Conscious Toxicity
Daria Hsu

daring yet vigilant together, to grow our family
and have happy children together - not to fear,
escape, attempt to return to the womb, to fail to be transparent
You promised me we'd travel the world and have
lots of babies together when you asked me to
marry me
So don't you cop out!

55.

Tell me dear:
When were we truly free?
Was it when my country was being ravaged and destroyed
By people with no conscience?[1]
Was it when I had to beg to join my classmates on
a school trip to Germany?[2]
Freedom is not true freedom
When it is not freedom for all
And so now, as we head into yet another lockdown,
Having escaped two previous ones in the US and in Europe
With a false sense of privileged victory,

Conscious Toxicity
Daria Hsu

Let's not just hide and hope for our own eventual escape to freedom
Let's speak up for freedom for others
Yes, even - or especially - the sheep
That believe themselves the safest when they're the least free
Needless to say, I won't beg for freedom on my knees
I will live and die standing up
If nothing else, I am courageous
I am a strong woman with a heart
I will live on my own terms
And I will fight for my right to die on my own terms -
Of COVID or of jabs -
The choice is solely mine

[1] I spent my youngest years in Russia, which during the 1990s, after the Perestroika, was being ravaged by various mafia clans and immoral opportunists.

[2] I grew up in the European Union as a non-EU citizen (or more specifically, in the Czech Republic as a Russian alien - "alien" being a very appropriate word for how I felt growing up there)

Conscious Toxicity
Daria Hsu

and suffered a lot of discrimination and even abuse, just one - milder - example being school trips to neighboring countries, during which my classmates could freely cross the border while I had to go through a lot of nerve-wracking screening and vetting of my travel application documents by the immigration police before I was allowed to participate in a trip.

56.

What purpose is there in a human life if its inherent dignity has been taken away by authority?
I'm compulsively cleaning and organizing the apartment yet again, as if hoping to regain some of the normalcy and control over my life that are being denied to me outside our four familiar walls
I feel hopeless, like there's nothing left to live for
All the joy and excitement I had entertained for fun summer plans with my family have been sucked out of me by an invisible but exceedingly strong death force: fun museums to take Zen to, restaurants to splurge at with Michael, and

Conscious Toxicity
Daria Hsu

Taiwan's small exotic islands that noone has heard of
Instead, I'm lying on the couch, breastfeeding Zen to sleep, having lost all my lust for the piles and piles of books I'd been meaning to read
I haven't published my monthly travel video - I'm two weeks behind but can't bring myself to do it
The angry blandness that has descended upon our town - or rather the willing greeting of this ugly perversity by locals - has me paralyzed,
Unsure where to escape because in some form, more or less, many around the globe seem to have succumbed to fear and conformity
In fact, I don't rush to leave
Exactly because both last times I left[1],
This ugliness caught up with me and with my dearest loved ones
This time I want to observe what's happening around me in hopes of gaining a new awareness,
And so, when the big, fat bus driver angrily lashes out, "Stop!" at me, signaling to put on my mask, I stop and put it on (defiantly, under my nose), and look him in the face all the way through the sad and angry little boy, maybe I even begin to see regret over how he just behaved (or maybe I just want to see it).

Conscious Toxicity
Daria Hsu

Soulful human connections and freedom are what turns this Earth into a paradise for all,
Yet perversely, children are being raised in isolation from each other, taught to fear contact and touch
Because their parents refuse to take responsibility for their pain and fears and instead follow TV propaganda to the T to distract themselves from their souls' duty to evolve
And this nastiness, I'm falling prey to it too...
I go outside, unmasked (it's now a 15000 Taiwan dollar offense to go unmasked!) among a crowd of followers - and I avoid looking at people's faces
Just after this lockdown started, I stopped looking people in the eyes
It's too painful to be stared at and angrily pointed at by strangers to put on my mask - but it's even more painful to look someone in the eyes only to find out moments later they've reported my nineteen-month-old for not complying to the fascist mask policies of the MRT[2]
So, what is it that I hope for?
I hope that staying here as opposed to fleeing I can practice finding my peace, love, and light no matter my surroundings (I'm certainly failing at that right now)

Conscious Toxicity
Daria Hsu

I hope for Zen to have a sibling (or siblings!) to play with and to spread light in this world
This world desperately needs light and consciousness and people who care

[1] We left the United States (California) and the Czech Republic to escape some of the Covid restrictions that we found nonsensical and oppressive, only to, eventually, find ourselves in a draconian-style lockdown in Taiwan.

[2] MRT is the public transportation system in Taipei

57.

Which part of myself do I need to bury
So I can move away from this wretched place?
I will not beg for oxygen and freedom -
You can send all the police and tank squads my way you want
Yet... even the bravest of hearts know fear,
And so does mine
Even the strongest of minds despair,
And so does mine -

Conscious Toxicity
Daria Hsu

How could it not when everyone here[1] is masked
up and following orders to the T
I am being reported to the police almost daily,
TV blasts rising virus cases,
And no one - not the organic supermarket vendor,
Not the egg seller,
Not even the police know when this will end,
But they all unanimously agree
That the promised June 8th,
For which a return to freedom had been scheduled,
is not coming
Third country[2], same regrettable spectacle
I used to think everything was negotiable except
for my freedom,
My freedom seemed so secure
It turns out freedom is negotiable too
When enough people allow it to be that way
Peaceful non-compliance is the solution
Don't comply
Be peaceful
Be peaceful
Don't comply
Stay lucid
Calm
At peace
Through all this madness

Conscious Toxicity
Daria Hsu

And if you want to cry
At how things are, don't hide your tears
Be kind
Speak up
Try not to lose your patience
I know it's easier said than done
Give all your loved ones a big hug
Especially those that don't comply either
They're making sure your kids and grandkids
Will walk this Earth in freedom
Although the ones that do comply
Are probably in biggest need of a hug
Ah, freedom!
It shall ring
From all rooftops yet again,
But this time freedom for all,
Truly for all it will be: humans and animals alike
Even plants! Yes, plants as well
For now, though, I am involuntarily
And unexpectedly caught up
In a social science experiment
A curious way to live,
But we'll adjust

[1] in Taiwan

Conscious Toxicity
Daria Hsu

[2] We lived in three countries during Covid: in the United States (California), then in the Czech Republic, and finally, in Taiwan (later returning to California via the Czech Republic)

58.

If this is not hell,
Then I am not sure what hell is,
Isolated from other humans,
With uncertain food supply,
But that is exactly where we are
Because I won't comply
I won't sell out my consciousness,
My precious soul, and my son's future
To the monstrosity that has been thrust upon us all
And with which everyone complies
My head is in a state of panic,
My hope is to escape to Russia,
My foreign motherland where we have not one
single friend or close family member
My hope is that it is free
I truly won't know until I see

Conscious Toxicity
Daria Hsu

I'm scared to move into a foreign land that is my motherland
This is not what I envisioned for myself:
I envisioned a spacious house with a large backyard and possibly a swimming pool
In an upscale neighborhood in California,
Surrounded by relatives, friends, and acquaintances,
But now the US seems like a godforsaken land,
Just like Europe, just like Taiwan
Is Russia the free escape I crave from my paralysis?

I'm imagining our complete isolation after, or rather if we move there
Michael doesn't speak Russian,
And people don't understand us,
Assuming that we are some annoying, rich American imperialists
That's what many people assume in Taiwan and in the Czech Republic, so why not there?

Michael asked me, if you had no escape, how would you raise your son in a happy environment?
His question is profound
I'm hoping to escape
Not as erratically as before

Conscious Toxicity
Daria Hsu

Not in a maniacal way
But just like before, my head is not mine anymore
as I'm frantically dreaming up escape routes
And refuse to lower my standards even by a bit
I demand a perfect, an ideal world,
Or else I refuse to live in it
I, fool! Witnessing pain and anger and insanity
pains me the same whether I see them in my
mother's or in the maskers' eyes
I know I cannot let my son be brutally hurt like I
was
Ironically, we are at home most days, in isolation -
which is the pain of my own childhood,
The lonely, bland existence between four walls
No one will meet us here because of the pandemic
We barely make it into the grocery store through
the mask police
I know it will be similar in the US
I naturally want to fight, to give my all to prevent
my son from living in this sick, dark regime,
But Michael had a point when he asked, what are
we teaching our son?
How long can I go on protecting Zen from
experiencing the pain of this world?
Am I truly just desperately trying to heal my own
unloved inner child?

Conscious Toxicity
Daria Hsu

Aren't we better off living in the world and
fighting for our freedoms?
Because whatever we escape,
Whatever we don't fight,
Our descendants will face tenfold
Where is the middle ground?
Do I just get off the couch and go out there into the
war zone, heckled, reported, yelled at angrily?
Take my son out somewhere reasonably peaceful
and less frequented by the angry, scared fascists?
Do I just leave our apartment for my son's sake
and go out despite my terror of doing so
Because I know he desperately needs fresh air
And his TV time is over the top in the past days
since the authorities closed down all indoor and
outdoor playgrounds?
Do I still go out with him, until the very, very end,
No matter what,
Until we are forced at gun point to stay in?
Until we crawl on our knees?
Where is the middle ground?

59.

Eternal sweat,

Conscious Toxicity
Daria Hsu

And I don't mean the thirty-eight-degree sweat of this summer
I mean eternal, ruthless, never-ending sweat,
A bloodbath of a sweat of barely ever getting a breather
From constantly running after our delightful, beloved precious son,
The friendliest, most sociable boy with the most adorable
And welcoming smile, the most heart-melting boy
Who waves at strangers like they're family and brings light into everyone's lives

But now everyone's masked up and goggled up,
Afraid of the virus or police or both,
Busy staring me down for going unmasked,
Remarking, reporting, angrily yelling at me to mask up
Now, there is no one left for our darling little boy to smile at and to share his light with
So smart he is
And wise beyond his twenty months!

No more play dates,
No more child and parent centers,
No more indoor playgrounds with fun names

Conscious Toxicity
Daria Hsu

Like Snoopy and Playtogether Forest,
No more slides, swings and ride-on horses in parks
No more
They've closed down everything a child loves
And parents look forward to for some much-
needed respite
They've taken that away from us
They've even tied knots in basketball hoops,
These sick, sick people

And so here we are, staying at home almost
twenty-four hours a day,
Unwilling to go out, there's not many places left to
go to,
And we can only take so much heckling and anger
from strangers
(We need to be stronger, I guess…)
And our poor boy, he must be losing his mind
His new friend is Cocomelon,
A cartoon friend to escape the blandness of a
childhood stolen
By adults in pain, surrounded by parents who are
exhausted,
Trying their best, but craving a breather too,
Who have their own pain, insecurities, fears, and
hopes

Conscious Toxicity
Daria Hsu

They're faced with,
We are the only people left in town to smile at,
Yet the smile has faded from our son's face -
That is the hardest, most painful pill to swallow
I am exhausted, overwhelmed
I can only play diner and dentist and pizza bakery
So many times - I crave some quiet moments to myself
My head is heavy like a kettle,
(Yes, like a kettle! My mother used to say that)
But I try to ignore it the whole day and just keep going
But for how long can we keep pushing, dear?
Both of us, tired, lonely, and at a crossroads,
Just a young couple with a child attempting to navigate,
Survive, daring to hope to thrive some day
Within this madhouse of a world

60.

Please God...
Lead my family and me
Into a safer place for us to live in,
Where we will feel at home and free,

Conscious Toxicity
Daria Hsu

And people will be kind
I want to break down and cry,
Having spotted to my surprise
Some growth, a nodule in my private parts
My immediate thought is cancer
My mom was always scared of cancer
Her father passed of an aggressive form
Of thyroid cancer in her youth,
So fast did he go from seemingly healthy to sick and dead
That the trauma of it has haunted her into her old age
My immediate heartbreak is of being separated overnight from my son
He breastfeeds and sleeps next to me each night
I can't, I don't want to imagine his heartbreak of me not being by his side when it's time to go to bed
All I ever wanted was to be his constant, never fading presence, the security he can count on any time no matter what
I'm shedding tears over the image of leaving my husband and son alone
Because I'm dead and buried,
My husband sitting on the couch,
Patiently feeding our son little chicken or fish pieces,

Conscious Toxicity
Daria Hsu

Lovingly encouraging him to eat,
While the TV screen is playing Cocomelon,
And me not being able to join them
Now with this health scare I wonder:
Maybe I haven't been living in the most authentic way?
I speak out about this totalitarian regime,
But have I been truly present with my husband?
I can't remember when
And with my son?
Rarely
I'm always on the go
Have to do this and that
Clean bathroom, read my books, take supplements,
have another baby, answer Facebook messages...
My life is one never-ending list
Of things to do and places to visit,
And for every one that I cross out,
I add three more
I do this to keep my life livable
Somehow without a list,
I am afraid I would be...
Lost? Bored? Without a purpose?
A large part of the list - travel -
Has lost its meaning as I've become cut off from
visiting places far and close

Conscious Toxicity
Daria Hsu

I'm in pain over what happened today,
Pedestrians finding out my address
And calling the police on me right in front of our house,
For standing at the entry of our home unmasked
Their angry lack of basic human love haunts me
How can anyone be so completely devoid of connection to another human being?
But me thinking about them all day,
Recording and posting a video of them,
Resisting them as Michael calls it,
And thus, gifting so much energy and time to these seemingly soulless beings,
Is that the most authentic way to live my life?
What do I hope to achieve?
Should I just put the mask under my chin when I'm outside so that noone can claim I don't mask up and go about my day?
A few days ago, Michael asked me "What would you want to do if you only had one month to live? What would truly resonate with your soul?"
Profound question
I'm off ~
To be with my family

Conscious Toxicity
Daria Hsu

61.

Ever since getting into a scuffle with the nasty,
pitiful maskers in front of our home and them
reporting me to the police,
I feel so uncomfortable passing by the small
businesses on our street
One of the guys who works there reported me to
the police despite himself having his mask under
his nose while he was calling police on me (he
made sure to fix it as I was recording him),
And the usually sweet dumpling lady looked at me
but didn't greet me back as I was passing by her
during the whole incident.
But anyway, since then, every time I walk through
our street, I feel such inner tension
I have been putting on a fake mesh mask since
then
And as I walked past those businesses today, I felt
like all eyes were on me
I took it down under my chin, then put it back over
my nose on purpose
To show them that their bitterness and anger and
reporting to the authorities have no effect on my
inner sense of freedom

Conscious Toxicity
Daria Hsu

And to simultaneously send the message "catch me if you can,"
My ego painfully aching under their imagined (or real, I dare not look in pride) judgmental stares
Why have I started putting on the fake mesh mask?
It was exhausting dealing with crap from every person that passes by us
The longer this goes on the scarier it feels to go against the grain
I guess something about that incident planted fear in me,
Even though the police never came knocking on our door,
Even though the police never fined us,
Even though the police themselves were much nicer
Then those bullies
My ego says not to put on my mask to trigger the heck out of the lame, scared followers
But I obviously crave peace, and want to go around my duties outside without being heckled, yelled at, reprimanded, and reported at every corner,
Without everyone blasting their bad vibes in my family's direction
I'm torn between complying and rebelling

Conscious Toxicity
Daria Hsu

My ego is what hurts the most
But also, there is pain from childhood,
Of being the outsider,
Of the humiliation of standing in the middle of the gym alone during PE class after the captains of two teams had picked even the fattest, slowest turtles for their teams - but not me, the last one to walk over to whichever team was uneven - to walk over completely humiliated, unloved, devastated on the inside - while acting like nothing much had happened, like I didn't even care
To be left out, stared at, disliked by my classmates every single time,
To be the one that doesn't belong,
The odd one out,
The one that doesn't fit in,
The disliked, strange one,
To hear ugly, nasty things about my country,
To be called a nerd in the most hateful tone of voice,
To feel completely out of place,
Like I don't belong here and yet it's not like I had a choice or anyone to protect me
Oh gosh, it brings tears to my eyes now that I think back to my journey from childhood through adolescence in the Czech Republic

Conscious Toxicity
Daria Hsu

Today I couldn't care less about their friendship or approval
My former bullies are probably stuck in a hole somewhere where they belong
It's a good question why some kids are so cruel, angry, and mean
Those kids (before the lockdown) always triggered the heck out of me at playgrounds when they interacted with Zen
I look at my son, he is objectively the sweetest, friendliest, most loving child,
But I have noticed that ever since this stupid lockdown,
He has changed
He used to smile and greet and wave at strangers,
But now barely anyone interacts with him on the street and even if they do,
He doesn't necessarily smile and wave back
He ignores them
His heart must have been broken by how people masked up and turned into scared, angry sheep overnight
Michael said a lady at the market reproached Zen for not wearing a mask and walked over to the other end of the stall lest our twenty-month-old spread the virus to her

Conscious Toxicity
Daria Hsu

When I was still unmasked, people would often walk in a half-circle around us to avoid me like the plague
And of course, Zen has witnessed all the angry reprimanding and reporting on the street
How can that not break a twenty-month-old's heart,
Inhibit his natural, sweet, socializing ways,
Break his trust in strangers?
(He has so much love in his heart and used to share it with random strangers on the bus, at restaurants, anywhere we'd go)
This regime which feeds off people's lack of love for each other, for humanity, for human interconnectedness and pathetic, medieval selfishness in attempts to survive a scary monster created by TV propaganda
Is destroying our children's hearts, lives, and future

62.

There is no shortcut,
Now I understand,
No easy straightforward way to happiness,

Conscious Toxicity
Daria Hsu

But patience, patience helps,
As do a heart filled with faith and love
And a soul filled with curiosity and peaceful
knowing that anything that comes one's way will
only serve to season and to grow,
And thus, only toward more peace and joy will
lead
It helps to know what truly matters
It's health, and love, light, and laughter in our
homes
And an educated, organized brain does help as
well,
But only if you have all the former
A brain itself can be misused, abused towards
supporting evil and inflicting lots of pain
If it is not profoundly interconnected with the
heart
But to a conscious soul, a totalitarian agenda is
nothing but a noise
Full of shit like a fly
Annoying like a mosquito
But one won't get lost in the depths of its
monstrosity
Just remember what matters the most in life, and
protect that smartly, wisely, at all costs
Work diligently on letting go of your ego

Conscious Toxicity
Daria Hsu

And you will be just fine
You're a spirit having a human experience
What doesn't kill you will season you and make
you so much stronger
You can find intense joy and light and peace even
in a lockdown, surrounded by madness
But have a plan B as well, don't be a fool
Buzz!
Slap
Wipe, wipe
Plop
Flush!

63.

How did it happen that, in a matter of days,
Our lives turned upside down?
The funny, or sad thing is that I no longer
remember how they used to be before,
Just a few weeks earlier,
Back when we were free
My heart breaks for Zen
I'm fine
I have been through everything and can survive

Conscious Toxicity
Daria Hsu

I've lived most of my life, up till now, a free
woman,
I've had a chance to make friends and build
relationships
Before this craziness started;
I have friends from college, and acquaintances
from here and there;
I know what it's like to walk around free,
unmasked and unafraid
(Or do I? At this point I am no longer sure...
It seems like such a distant past at this point:
Like a past life,
Like decades ago -
Yet it's been just a year and a few months since this
craziness started...)
Anyway, I'm fine
I'm married! With a child
I've built my life
But Zen! What about Zen?
I'm worried about him
Of course, he is heartbroken
And slow to build trust with strangers
(He can't say it yet, but I think I can sense him
becoming more serious, somber, or sad, beyond a
toddler's age)

Conscious Toxicity
Daria Hsu

Maybe I'm just reading my own worries and aches into him that he does not have? I grew up feeling very isolated and lonely
After all, Michael says Zen is fine! He is his happy self
Yes, he still laughs with us
We try to do our very best to entertain him and create a joyful, safe space for him to grow, basically trying to isolate him from these double-masked, goggled up, face shielded, robotically-rule-following people who have not a single clue about the meaning of "dissent" or "non-compliance", who take things at face value and can't put two and two together, that if everyone is following rules to the T, almost everything is closed, almost everyone is staying home (the streets are so empty that if I had been transplanted here from the past and didn't know what was going on, I'd have thought it's because of nuclear Holocaust or medieval plague), yet according to the TV the numbers of infected are still growing fast and out of control - there's something rotten in the kingdom of Taiwan
In a big country, you can trick people with these lies, but on a small island where everyone dances to the same drum beat or is violently oppressed

Conscious Toxicity
Daria Hsu

and excommunicated with nowhere to go, you'd
think these lies are powerless
They are not
The TV continuously casts spells upon these
islanders and they are bewitched!
Anyway, me, I'm fine
I'm from steel, bring it on – what doesn't kill me
makes me stronger
And I have already built my life – my marriage,
family, friends, acquaintances – in the unmasked,
(seemingly) free past
But it's Zen I'm worried about
It's Zen my heart breaks for, bleeds for!
What an isolating experience it must be being
cooped up at home with mom and dad
continuously, and when we do go out to witness
fearful, anxious, angry people whose faces he
cannot see and who constantly keep telling us to
put on a mask (or a shirt) on him and get visibly
nervous or agitated at the sight of our twenty-
month-old piece of pure yummy goodness and
delight running around the empty mall unmasked
and – oh, how dare he?! – nibbling on a blood rice
cake in-between
Because in a pandemic, children no longer need to
eat and play, right?

Conscious Toxicity
Daria Hsu

At the local organic store, the employee literally
told Michael we shouldn't be feeding Zen when
we're out and about
I got so angry inside I wanted to slap that bitch
back to her senses but instead I simply rolled Zen's
stroller out of the store as soon as possible while
Michael stayed on to warn her about the possible,
dangerous side effects of the vaccines for the virus
blown out of proportion
He said she was open to hearing him out and
exclaimed, "Oh?"
But it's not even about the vaccines and Michael
knows that - in fact, he was the one who first
voiced it: it's about unresolved human pain being
projected onto a virus
It's about the thirst for global control which again
comes out of pain
It's about our society being completely
disconnected, not falling apart and still
functioning only because of either violently forced
conformity that completely breaks a person's soul,
free will, and ability to see outside the box
(welcome to Taiwan) or because of stuffing oneself
to the brim with antidepressants and anxiety meds
and sedatives and sleeping pills and then going out
into the world all smiley and happy while fuming

Conscious Toxicity
Daria Hsu

or shattered or completely lost deep inside
(welcome to America)
Anyway, I'm worried about Zen living in such an isolated existence
Even our family friend O, with whom Michael's mom grew up as a little girl and who has a lasting connection both to her and Michael's uncle, who has hosted us many times in his home - even he
has denied his hospitality to us from now on
And his granddaughter A was Zen's last remaining playmate here in Taipei, they got along so well, she adored him and he used to be mightily entertained and laugh so heartily with her
His last remaining playmate gone...
Due to the adults in her life lost to fear, paranoia, anxiety, pain
Michael told them gently but honestly how we feel about this scamdemic and here we go:
We lost our last connection, and Zen has no more children to play with
It doesn't help that the government has banned more than five people from gathering indoors
But Zen and A could have played while her parents are working - the rule could have been worked around if O had wished so

Conscious Toxicity
Daria Hsu

But clearly, he fears the virus and maybe also
being reported by his neighbors if he invites us
over
Locals here are pros at reporting non-compliers to
the police
The machine is well oiled and running strong
I am worried about Zen
How is he going to build friendships and get
married?
We need to bring him to an environment that is
closer to normal
And I really, really want him to have a sibling or
siblings close in age so they can have each other
and play together no matter what is happening in
the world
So that he, they don't grow up feeling isolated and
lonely like I did
Please, God, send us a sweet, little, lovely, healthy,
happy sibling for Zen to be loved by him and to
love him in return
Or more siblings, the more the merrier!
And please together with our bundle of sweet,
radiant joy send me and Michael a lot of patience
and courage and strength and good health,
endurance and stamina and mental emotional
clarity and peace, and still some free time too for

Conscious Toxicity
Daria Hsu

relaxing, unwinding, and following our dreams
(Michael needs that, a lot of time to himself -
which means I need extra mental and emotional
endurance and patience)
Please, dissipate any worries or fears I and Michael
may be feeling about having another child and
help us recognize the blessing that growing our
family constitutes
After all, in this madness, it is within our family
that we find joy, comfort, peace, light, and
laughter! Please God, watch over our family -
thank you for always doing so
It ain't always easy, but I know you are always by
our side shining your radiant, glorious light and
all-forgiving love over us
Amen

64.

I feel like I have aged a thousand years,
But in a way that feels good
I look at photos of your family,
I used to want so much to be like them,
To be them almost,
Rich, successful, well off California dwellers,

Conscious Toxicity
Daria Hsu

Lots of siblings, close, on good terms,
Meeting up for dinners and lunches,
Spending lovely family time together,
No drama or arguments or tears,
Just nice clean multi-story houses,
Organic gardens and tasty food,
No open disagreements,
Tactful (or tense?) avoidance of the topic,
Or acceptance of each other, because... they're family!
They all got vaccinated, they all put on their masks
Now they all dine at restaurants again after the reopening
They seem to go with the flow and be unsinkable,
Gathered around the table dining on fine restaurant foods
As if the whole pandemic had never happened
I wouldn't want to be them
From every hardship we have been through,
I have grown
I have seen what I would never have seen had I stayed behind
But somewhere deep inside a tiny doubtful voice asks,
What now? Are we the fools after all?
Having skipped from country to country,

Conscious Toxicity
Daria Hsu

Avoided lockdowns only to have ended up in the craziest, most fascist one of them all,
Having worked and worried our asses off about the documents for Taiwan,
Only to now be planning to leave before even finishing the last - meant-to-be easy - step: live here
I can feel myself becoming increasingly possessive of Zen and Michael the longer we stay isolated
What am I doing daring to separate Zen from his yeye and nainai who love him so much?
Just to have them all to myself,
Just to not have to get triggered by my mother-in-law and rich relatives,
Planning to homeschool out of a sudden desire to completely isolate and insulate our son from any pain (and there's a lot out there),
Trying to give him a sibling so he doesn't feel lonely like I used to as a child
But doesn't he need family and friends?
They're there! In California!
But I want to live my way,
To not feel controlled by anyone,
To not financially depend on my parents-in-law
I'm set on being independent,
On making it on our own,

Conscious Toxicity
Daria Hsu

But at what cost to my son's and husband's well-being?
At what point is it too much?
I'm set on making it on our own, to push ourselves to see how far we can make it,
To build our own life, our very own life
I want to be the one in control,
The revered popo of the family,
The Mrs Hsu,
The matriarch
Am I reliving my mother's possessive painful dream?
She ended up alone and isolated from everyone including me, her daughter
She just has her husband and son to herself,
Like I'm clinging to Zen and Michael at all costs
She's in control and so am I
Am I reliving my mother's life?
I think I am...
Oh, help me God!
When our California relatives find out we're off to Russia without even having received our Taiwan documents,
When all of them find out,
They will surely judge us

Conscious Toxicity
Daria Hsu

They will surely disapprovingly and quietly think that we are crazy,
That we don't know where we're headed
This is not what serious, well-to-do, successful Asian Californians do after all
They stay close to family and become programmers and accountants,
Which I now understand is a remnant, a mirror image of the culture we are currently in,
Which adopts and follows fascist rules without thought and without questioning
I will speak my true thoughts at the expense of sounding bitter, judgmental, and jealous
I dread Michael's parents' reaction upon finding out that we're moving to Russia,
Or is it the projection of my own parents that I dread?
Maybe a combination of both
What if we come to Russia
And it is fucking lonely and poor
With bitter unfriendly judgmental people?
Then we will be the biggest fools of all
But not to see, not to give it a chance would be a sin
God will carry us through on his loving wings

Conscious Toxicity
Daria Hsu

65.

I no longer remember what it was like to live free
here in Taiwan
Even though I walked these same streets,
It feels like a past life!
Now I am uncomfortable, fearful to even leave the
house
In the past half a year we have lived it up:
Snoopy Play Center was paradise - not just for kids
but for adults! I would have loved to return into
this heaven for youthful fun-loving souls!
Love Family was crowded, with questionable food,
but the indoor Ferris wheel was unique and fun for
me and Zen to ride on!
Playtogether... So many memories... Our favorite
place! There should be a lovely Playtogether with
chill vibes in every town on this planet
Hotel rooftop pool for Mother's Day and Victory
Over Fascism Day - we are far from victorious but
we were so lucky to spend one of our very last
weekends of Taiwanese freedom splashing around
above the city and eating our hearts out at the
hotel buffet!
Buffets are closed

Conscious Toxicity
Daria Hsu

Indoor dining is closed
Playgrounds are closed
Eating and drinking on the streets is banned
Minime ... Our last step into the faint remainder of
freedom... An empty children's play area with us
the second and last customers of the day
It used to be a lively place in prior months...
They closed Minime too

There is a virus,
But there is no pandemic
The "pandemic" has been announced globally by
politicians - not epidemiologists,
While secretly the process of counting the infected
has been switched to a new method of counting
millions of those that display no symptoms but test
positive,
And it is well known by doctors that the tests have
an up to forty percent chance of a false positive,
Which means that we have been set up for a
"pandemic" which will never end
Because there will always be false positives
As long as they force everyone to test
Test or inject to go to the hairdresser,
Test or inject to swim in a pool,
Inject to keep your job,

Conscious Toxicity
Daria Hsu

Inject to get a job
A system fueled by terror instilling propaganda,
Carrot for complying,
Stick for rebelling
We won't be free,
Our children won't be free
While we all feel and are healthy,
Don't you see?
The system has been set up in a way which
precludes its return to our freedom
People around the globe need to wake up to its
deceit and terror
And then things will begin to change for the better

66.

Don't you think, dear, that we are free?
Don't you dare think that we are free,
Or else if you do, you will be sorely disappointed
Don't you think, dear, that it's just California, just
Canada, just Australia?
Don't you dare think it's just your state or just your
country,
Or else if you do, you will be sorely disappointed

Conscious Toxicity
Daria Hsu

Guess what: it's California, and the Czech
Republic, it's Israel, Taiwan, and Moscow too
This cancer has no respect for countries' borders
No sitting on park benches, no eating or drinking
outside, no children sliding down and swinging,
no teens shooting basketball hoops, no stylish
haircuts or summer frolicking in swimming pools
without proof of vaccination or test
No vaccine? No grocery shopping at the market
No vaccine? No school for your children
No vaccine? Mask up, you infected lowlife, or else
you cannot enter
Scanning your temperature and collecting your
information is no longer enough to enter
Taiwanese outdoor markets and grocery stores
We've become numbers now
The last digit on our ID determines when we get to
shop for food and when not
I am a five, odd-numbered,
And Michael is a zero, even-numbered
We are no longer allowed to shop together as a
family
I used to tell Michael that morning shopping with
him and Zenny at the Muzha outdoor market was
my favorite activity
No more of that for us

Conscious Toxicity
Daria Hsu

Believe me, I tried to fight
Yesterday, I took Zen into my arms and broke through the police barricade
Two (or three?) policemen weren't enough - the uniformed masked-up cowards had to call in back-up on me
They were shoving me and Zen around the market, egging on Michael in Chinese to grab and drag me out of the market
The cowards were afraid to get too violent with me in such a public place where everyone was staring and recording (I was recording everything myself) so they egged on my husband to physically assault me
The female police supervisor, upon hearing Michael's response, "I cannot do that. That is physical abuse," replied, "No, that's not physical abuse"
Can you believe that? A woman invested with power and authority directing a husband to physically assault his own wife and drag her out of an outdoor market
How have humans sunk so low? Why do we allow lowlifes to write laws for us and exercise authority over our families? Why do we reward the sickest

Conscious Toxicity
Daria Hsu

of the sick with promotions and invest them with
power over our families?
The cowards called the police (I thought they were
here to protect and serve us?), took our ID's,
angrily yelled at me at the top of their lungs,
"DON'T BE RUDE!", kept looking something up on
their phones and calling their colleagues
I was standing right there in front of the barricade
face-to-face with these cowards, recording their
faces - faces of followers, followers of brutality,
thoughtless and angered by any digression from
brain-dead application of orders from above
I was holding Zen in my arms under the large
tent-like umbrella that cowards had installed at the
outdoor market entrance to protect themselves
from the scorching tropical sun
The cowards were uncomfortable with my
presence right by the barricade, right in their faces
They moved the tent all the way behind the
barricade so that Zen and I were forced to move
further away from them into shade - or get a
heatstroke
They are comfortable with enforcing draconic,
heartless, and immoral rules over citizens
But turn into pussies when looking into my eyes
and divert their stares sideways

Conscious Toxicity
Daria Hsu

(At least they didn't beat me up
Don't mess with American police
Or Czech police for that matter
I wouldn't want to break any police barricades in those "democracies")
Now we're numbers
Just that: numbers
I've cried a thousand tears over this, but truly -
what can I do? I'm a five, my husband is a zero,
our son is a seven
And newly, odds and evens are not allowed to mix
We shop separately - or if we refuse to comply, we will get heavily fined or go to jail
Is there any other option for all of us but to bend down to this perversity, this sickness, this cancer of society?

67.

My head hurts,
A kettle of trauma and perception, sensitivity,
A silent panic rises within me
For weeks, months,
Maybe secretly for years I have been wondering
Did I end up on the right planet?

Conscious Toxicity
Daria Hsu

Darling, we must be from the future
And came into the now to save the people here
from their suicidal course
How else to explain the immense unspoken and
unacknowledged pain within families and societies
on this Earth,
And everyone going around their everyday tasks
In a psychotic way, pretending like there isn't that
huge fucking rot eating at them and everyone
around them alive,
Acting la-di-da,
They suffer a lot - behind closed doors

Once that door is shut,
The truth comes out,
All hell breaks loose
We break down, manipulate,
Abandon, scream, become passive aggressive,
Get overwhelmed with anger,
Switch between complete panic and total apathy
We torture ourselves, our loved ones,
Our children in the most hideous, heinous ways,
And then we leave our house in the morning
And engage in the most preposterous theater

Conscious Toxicity
Daria Hsu

Good thing if we are at least conscious of how
crappy we feel and all the crap that just went on in
our home earlier,
That's a good start,
There's potential to get somewhere,
To wake up from the collective unconsciousness
God save those who genuinely believe they're
doing well,
Those are the truly lost ones,
The ones that appear and think they got it all
under control
Once the tower begins to crumble
They will turn into the whiniest, most frightened
babies
Collective unconsciousness is the true mental
illness
We think of the schizophrenic stepmother or the
cuckoo homeless guy or the student with ADHD,
But those are all scapegoats - the sacrificial lambs
of our society -
Labeled, blamed, drugged, abused,
In order for us to continue avoiding our own sick
shadow, collective and individual - the true
disorder, cancer, virus
The schizophrenics, the depressives, the bipolars
have a head start on us all

Conscious Toxicity
Daria Hsu

No matter how misdiagnosed, misunderstood, mislabeled,
They know at least that something's wrong with them,
And if they're brave enough to unplug from the system - the money-hungry pharma's drugs - and to power through,
They're right on the path towards salvation
While the "normal" ones keep on their path of painful, delusional denial

And please, let us already stop pathetically pretending that the Second World War (and any other wars and genocides) was an outlier,
As if everyone had been innocently, peacefully picking flowers and suddenly - boom - the evil Nazis came and destroyed millions
The Nazi is within,
Hitler (and Stalin) are in you
To have gotten to the point of totalitarian brutality, of war,
A whole lot of shit must have been going down in people's hearts and minds and homes,
The individual and collective crazy simply accumulated, built up to the point of no return

Conscious Toxicity
Daria Hsu

Where an explosion was the only hope at waking up delusional, self-lying, abused, abusive flower pickers.
Why doesn't anyone talk about that?
Because it's easier to act like something big and evil came down upon us,
Like we are no part of it,
To act like innocent, shocked bystanders who just happened to be picking flowers in the vicinity

A new age of rage is upon us
So it is doubly important to understand that if it has gotten to the point of segregation, social exclusion, reporting on each other, mutilated bodies, destroyed businesses and lives -
And the majority has no qualms over witnessing all this, participating and enforcing -
There must be a whole lot, lot, lot of unacknowledged pain going on within the hearts and minds of seemingly innocent, complying bystanders
Their hearts are being eaten alive by dark rot as they are double-masking, reprimanding, and reporting on others, embracing and enforcing authoritarianism anywhere and everywhere

Conscious Toxicity
Daria Hsu

The successful ability to scapegoat and misuse a
group of people or an animal virus in order to
quickly and without a significant backlash institute
a totalitarian regime testifies of this planet's
emotional and mental illness
You don't need a doctor's PhD
You simply need to wake up now and see

68.

Where will we end up?
I'm scared
I don't know
In this cruel, painful world,
There seems to be no free, familiar, peaceful place
to settle down - affordable and kind to all
We're going to Russia in less than two weeks,
But this time around I'm very clear that it's no
escape
Most people believe in the psychotic virus
propaganda,
Playgrounds are closed off,
Authorities have no qualms over introducing
forced vaccines

Conscious Toxicity
Daria Hsu

They have started with service employees and teachers,
But nothing is stopping them from forcing everyone
It is official news now: they are working on standardizing vaccine passports around the world - to create a global uniform one that will shut out anyone who refuses the mandatory injection from education, services and freedom of movement
It's scary when there is nowhere left to escape,
And even if we do find a more peaceful place,
There is no guarantee this perversity, destructive anti-human ungodly cancer won't reach our "safe" hideout by the time our son grows up
Eventually Zen will need to move out, spread his wings, follow his soul's calling, fall in love, and build a family of his own -
How will he do all of this in an unfree, totalitarian world possesses by devil, human pain, and unconsciousness?
I admit I no longer see the light in this world,
And that is probably the scariest, most hopeless fact of all
I am one fearful, anxious mama,
A ball of confusion, panic, at a loss for words, red-eyed, utterly unsure as I spend countless sleepless

Conscious Toxicity
Daria Hsu

night driving myself crazy trying to figure out a path to eternal safety
There seem to be no path and guarantees
Out of all the impressive education I have received - and I am especially grateful for the countless discussions on freedom of thinking and warnings of fascism in the German schools I attended - I still find myself sitting here on the kitchen chair, breastfeeding and only half-present with my son, and at a complete loss as to how to build our lives - puzzled and scared
The best I can think of is to live day-by-day - but how do we settle down, choose a place to buy a house, grow and raise our family if we live day-by-day with no guarantees of freedom and safety? To continue to live bravely - not just exist, not just survive - to live out our souls' vibrant dreams within totalitarianism and not to get hopeless and depressed over our son's uncertain, potentially completely unfree future is the biggest challenge of all…

69.

I have a son I really, really love,

Conscious Toxicity
Daria Hsu

Who is my all,
And if you have someone worth fighting for,
You're blessed
You reach a point where you have been slapped
and apprehended so many times
You begin to lose your fear over what others think,
How others will react,
Whether they will disapprove and abandon you
Many, most others are nothing but walking,
stalking robots programmed not to think for
themselves but follow,
Programmed to believe in this society's infallible
"truths,"
Shells over severe pain left undealt with,
But if you know the meaning of true love,
If you see it every day in your child's eyes,
And if your bread and roof don't immediately
depend on the rotting, perverse system,
You have no excuse not to speak up,
To safely and peacefully non-comply
Don't let bullshitters off the hook -
Give them hell back whenever appropriate
Speak up
Many think what you think but they're afraid:
Afraid to lose their job, or to be fined, to lose
connections with family and friends

Conscious Toxicity
Daria Hsu

Speak up for them
Many think what you think but feel isolated, being surrounded by propaganda
Speak up for them
Many feel that something's off, something's rotten in this uncivil civilization but can't quite put it into words
Speak up for them
Over the past month, I feel like I've aged years, decades even
I used to have idealistic dreams
Now they're all destroyed
I still have ways to go: to live with no faith and trust in humans is isolating and no way to live long-term
But I see humans' pain much more clearly now: their anger, grand self-lies, and self-delusion, their uncanny willingness to follow
Indeed, there seems to be in humans something robotic
Until they wake up, that is, and reconnect with their souls and bloom upon this gorgeous Earth
Of course I am afraid
I'm often terrified!

Conscious Toxicity
Daria Hsu

But if I lean into my higher self, I can rest assured that it will guide me - with the kind help of my guardian angels and spirit guides
I'm no longer as afraid as I used to be to look severely injured, deranged people in the eye, to speak up against sick, traumatizing behaviors and rules
If I don't, who will?
If you don't, who will?
I feel like I have grown a thousand wrinkles
I am exhausted and near my breaking point,
But I am ready to keep going and grow a million more,
If it means a free and vibrant future for my son
If I muzzle up myself and him and remain anxiously silent,
What kind of mother would I be?
I'll take up the fight and gladly accept the wrinkles that come with it - they're but an outwardly manifestation of growing wisdom, resilience, courage, and peace,
But I also must remind myself to not get lost in the outer world so much as to forget spending quality time with Zen - that is the most precious time on Earth, time with Michael and Zen - those moments of goofiness and laughter, games and

Conscious Toxicity
Daria Hsu

conversations, and more goofy laughter are
precious, and I must remain present in them and
enjoy them fully rather than be distracted by my
anxious and depressive thoughts
After all, it's so that these moments may continue
and multiply to no end in the coming years,
decades, and centuries that I face challenges, fight
back with peaceful noncompliance and speak up

70.

How many hooplas and ooplas do I need to go
through to get this house?
At least I get a chance to go through them -
Many never get that chance
The system is not broken as some may claim
It is a perfectly oiled machine of oppression with
roots reaching centuries back,
Maybe forever back in human history
In which it is not a given that families have a right
to a roof over their heads,
In which young adults face homelessness way too
often
Having a home is a privilege

Conscious Toxicity
Daria Hsu

In this system it helps to act successful and well-off,
Even if you're barely making ends meet
It helps to act composed, friendly, and upbeat, not too emotional, not raw,
To be well-groomed,
Hair combed, new-ish looking clothes are helpful too
Profitable bank statements and fat cash reserves are the determining factor between who gets a mysterious nod of approval and who gets mercilessly thrown like a dog to this society's outskirts
Being "white" is probably helpful too
I wouldn't know for sure because I can't compare: I've never been "black"
I've felt "black" on many occasions in my life though,
And that, coupled with my expanding awareness of a multitude of ways in which we ignore, accept, and even welcome oppression in all corners of the world, leaves little doubt in me that something so superficial as a label of "skin color" would serve as yet another excuse to subjugate and rule

Conscious Toxicity
Daria Hsu

But don't focus on the external oppressor at the
expense of the vilest and least talked about
oppression: the one that happens in our homes
Michael always tells me this
It is profoundly true:
Oppression from our parents, parental figures, and
grandparents, teachers, neighbors, and strangers
on the streets, on city trams and inside subways
cars:
The shushes, hushes, the sideway disapproving
stares, the gaslighting of how we feel as children,
the lack of ears ready to listen to how we feel and
what it is we want, the readiness to call us spoiled
and rowdy and loud and disobedient and lazy,
impossible and difficult and attention seeking, the
expectation of us to be good, little, quiet robots that
complete all homework on time and follow the
schedule and society's questionable and oppressive
rules and norms even if the world is crumbling
down, the "control your child" and finger wiggles
and fear of "spoiling" and raising a "monster" due
to giving too much attention and affection - that is
the deepest, sickest oppression of them all
And so, while I tremble in fear without having
stolen or killed about whether we will be approved

Conscious Toxicity
Daria Hsu

for modern-day slavery called a thirty-year mortgage -
Because enslaving ourselves in that way is the only chance for our family to have a roof over our heads -
I remind myself that I am not crazy for having mixed feelings about the prospect of a first new home for my family and nausea about the sickening process of being forced to seek a blessing of approval from modern-day slave owners before they maybe, possibly relent and accept me and my family into a thirty-year servitude in exchange for a two-bedroom, two-bathroom fixer-upper cabin on a reasonably sized sloping up lot in the Southern California mountains
And I know that all forms of oppression have a good chance of ending on our Earth when we begin pursuing radical, unapologetic self-love, self-acceptance, self-forgiveness, saying a firm loving no to oppression from our parents, when we no longer accept being spoon-fed by society all the big and little white lies that are meant to keep us in compliant apathy and instead, we demand to measure up all that we witness to the vibrations of our all-loving, all-knowing hearts

Conscious Toxicity
Daria Hsu

Let us stop caring about being good little actors in the well-oiled machine of destructive collective insanity and begin to take an honest, egoless, critical look at ourselves and our homes

If we can learn to see through bullshit there, seeing through the bullshit of political and corporate systems, of mainstream and social media will seem easy-peasy

Because truly only one who isn't conscious of the gaslighting one has been subjected to throughout childhood and adulthood and continues to subject own children and grandchildren to within the privacy of home is able to fall deeply for totalitarian, fear-mongering, carrot-and-stick games, and divide-and-conquer strategies

When we stop projecting onto outside oppressors (not deny them, just stop projecting) and critically engage with the sick bullshit in our childhood homes and current homes, we will finally have a chance at positive change

Thank you, my loveliest husband, for helping me become conscious of this

71.

Conscious Toxicity
Daria Hsu

"Мамочки родненькие, как я устала…"[1]

As I was trying to cast a prosperity spell this early afternoon,
I realized how completely exhausted I was,
How I have neglected myself, forgotten about myself, have denied myself a single caress, no personal time, no breather… For two months I haven't meditated, I haven't been alone in my own sweetness (and sadness) for two long months
This battle, maybe I am no longer fit for it? I was wondering as I was breastfeeding Zen
All I had asked for was some uninterrupted time to cast a spell, maybe some me time as well, some time to meditate and align with my highest self,
But even that was denied to me,
The very little I had asked for was broken,
And I felt violated all throughout
So, I stormed out and lashed out
There is no easy solution with Michael unwilling to hear me, or to respect my magical side and need for complete privacy and quiet when I engage in a battle of white light and manifestation for my family
He can be judgmental in what he disapproves of in me

Conscious Toxicity
Daria Hsu

And sometimes fails to understand the importance
of certain things to me in the moment
I know that if he had explicitly asked for some
quiet time for a task,
I would not get on the phone with someone (for
him, it's always his parents...) and let Zen bang the
heck out of the door and yell at him through the
door, "MICHAEL!! MICHAEL!!!" as he is trying to
concentrate
I would take Zenny aside and redirect him gently
to one of a multitude toys and games in our home,
I would hang up the conversation with my parents
for a starter,
And focus on my sleepy milk-thirsty son's well-
being while his mama wraps up her personal time
But no, it did not occur to my hubby to do that
He instead kept on chatting with his parents while
his poor son was about to break through the door
to mama,
So I stormed out of my square and circle
formations,
Fed up with having to listen to his phone chatter
while I tried to cast a spell,
Barely, amateurishly creating a spiritual exit and
entry door to my formation,

Conscious Toxicity
Daria Hsu

And yelled at him that what he was doing was unacceptable
Honestly, his parents and his devotion to them to the point of getting lost in the space-time continuum irks me quite a bit
His mom's toxic refusal to keep her million insecurities and fears in check and instead spewing them onto our heads irks me,
As does his dad's overly quiet, constipatingly non-emotional demeanor with the only emotion he is comfortable displaying being anger
Like dude, yes, you're rich and you own a pharmacy where you inject people with experimental vaccines nowadays, but you're not a Chinese emperor so you can get off you high horse and talk a bit more freely and get help for your anger, for God's sake, and maybe explore the rainbow of all the other emotions
And yes, of course I come out of my own bitterness and my mom's dislike of her own in-laws who openly disliked and bullied her,
And of course, I'm possessive of my son around them in questionable ways,
But I can also smell some serious bullshit in those people who are now my family,

Conscious Toxicity
Daria Hsu

And his Northern California cousins are so lost to the narrative that one of them openly refused to let Zenny play with her daughter indoors unless we inject ourselves with an experimental vaccine

That J-witch is wicked and you know what Michael's dad did when she voiced that sick rule of hers to us? He got angry at me and told me how I am so close-minded (something about looking only at a horse's tail instead of the whole body or along those lines) and otherwise kept quiet, didn't beep a word to the dear cousin about how she was traumatizing his own grandson by denying him seeing and playing with his second cousin without being jabbed

He just kept wining and dining her in his own kitchen and then went on to inject the only Taiwanese people who were openly suspicious about the scam

So, you see, I'm not a big fan of Michael's parents and his somewhat too-close relationship with them - he has no friends to call, or maybe he does but doesn't really try - just his parents, his toxically anxious and insecure mom and authoritarian, angry dad

They're not all bad - neither am I,

Conscious Toxicity
Daria Hsu

But I like soulful connections and these people seem to exist on a different plane from which I'm not accessible to them and they to me - maybe I don't want to be - maybe despite all my parents have done to me I still feel closer to them - of course I do, I grew up with them and we forgive our parents way too easily
Ah, parents, those creatures!

[1] "Dear Lord, how tired I am..."

72.

I don't know what can be said in light of what is happening
I sometimes wonder if I'm delusional, quietly deranged
They are fighting a dangerous virus that spreads like fire and kills like plague
They are sane: they get the vaccine, put masks on their children, and take them to Disneyland and kids' museums where their children interact with others' children and play in water and laugh
While I, I... What am I doing here? Rebelling pointlessly against a system,

Conscious Toxicity
Daria Hsu

Reading Russian, Czech, American news and
growing hopeless, panicky, depressed,
And our son is cooped up at home on many days,
With no human interaction except us two
I've been called angry, an extremist by people I call friends,
Even if they are wrong - who am I, Daria, to stand up to authorities around the world? I am a mere ant in the course of human history
To me, my fight for my son's freedom is everything, my all,
But let's face it - the world remains the same
It doesn't hear my plea to remember how to love each other fearlessly
In Russia they're building concentration camps for the "infected" - they look like Auschwitz to me
I've visited Auschwitz, and Theresienstadt, and Sachsenhausen
I can tell a hospital from a concentration camp
These are no hospitals
Russians say, people are quiet and don't protest because they are afraid, because they don't know their rights, because they have been divided into two groups (vaxxed and unvaxxed) and conditioned to fight each other like angry, homeless dogs, загрызть друг другу глотку[1]...

Conscious Toxicity
Daria Hsu

Without proof of vaccine, Russian people are no longer allowed to fly on planes, study at universities, work, visit restaurants, they may even be denied from buses and trains
In Russia the new cryptic "evacuation" law of June first twenty-twenty-one prescribes death marches for residents of "disaster areas:" hundreds of people will be forced to march for one to one-and-a-half hours, then allowed a ten-to-fifteen-minute break, then march again all day with a longer break of up to one-and-a-half hours in the second half of the day
Those who don't march will be transported in freight cars, dump trucks, and... Passenger trains
This is for evacuation from war zones and disaster areas
Oh God, I don't understand: where are they supposed to march and why?
It's strange, the grimmer the news from Russia, the more immune I become to it
My consciousness gently switches from analytical newspaper reading to perceiving the news as if it were an excerpt from a World War Two memoir
After all, this is too grim for a human heart to read and acknowledge as really happening - right now, as I am sitting wrapped up in my warm blanket on

Conscious Toxicity
Daria Hsu

a couch - to people who are very real and whom I can in no way help

I have been accused by my so-called friends of dwelling on the negative, of feeding the negative by spreading this news on social media,

But people must know, Americans who choose to wear a mask must know that for us here in Taiwan - on concrete streets in thirty-eight-degree Celsius temperatures - it is not a choice, it is a law enforced by police

Czechs who choose to turn a blind eye to hotels, restaurants, museums, swimming pools, gyms denying access to unvaccinated people and survive in their bubble of spirituality or take "just these two jabs towards freedom" need to realize that no amount of injections in the world will lead them to freedom

I'm torn between the very real realization that what is happening is ugly, sick, the opposite of "love thy neighbor as thyself" and my preoccupation with darkness, my fantasies of Anne Frank's destiny, I can almost smell the death from those articles I'm reading

But I'm ashamed to admit my fantasies and that smell were there before this harmless little virus took over our planet,

Conscious Toxicity
Daria Hsu

And in that sense, I am part of the problem and not the solution,
In that sense, my friends are right that dwelling on darkness breeds darkness,
But so does remaining silent
An unpleasant virus has uncovered a deeper, much more dangerous illness in humanity: the painful monsters we've held onto and hidden in family closets, the lack of love for our fellow humans (and animals and plants!) - that universal, unshakable, honest, forgiving love that resonates from Earth to heaven and makes our hearts skip beats and rejoice when we catch glimpses of it in ourselves and others - and our complete disregard for our own freedom - freedom to think, freedom to choose, freedom to share our thoughts without being monitored, labeled extremist, deleted
Who have we become?
Angry, anxious, brain and soul-dead ghouls who'd rather give up on seeing ever again their unvaccinated "loved" ones than risk being human, that beautiful condition that includes the tiny, faint possibility of death from a virus
It's not too late to wake up, brave up, love up
It's not too late to realize that it's time to seriously renegotiate our contract with authorities

Conscious Toxicity
Daria Hsu

worldwide - whether it be Moscow's mayor or a California highway patrol officer
If they no longer serve us, they don't deserve our money nor our faith
You heard me: no taxation without representation
Don't you despair or give it up
Step out of the box and think of solutions that can lead to the renewal that mankind absolutely needs: decentralized currency? Remote modest lifestyles with own gardens? Homeschooling communities?
I'm sure once you begin, you'll find solutions more brilliant than I could ever imagine

[1] slit each other's throats

73.

Although outside battles can be challenging indeed,
It is the battles within ourselves, within our family homes that are the most challenging of all
To survive the month of July twenty-twenty-one, Oh boy, what a challenge!
I instinctively know what is best: to just be,
To enjoy the here and now, to go to the park,

Conscious Toxicity
Daria Hsu

To get boba milk tea, to view nature, to ponder
over the river,
To smile at and fuss over Zenny in a motherly way,
But around me there is a hurricane of
unpredictability,
Road blockages coupled with Michael's desperate
angry pushiness
To construct our life exactly according to his
imagination:
Crestline, two bedrooms, no more than hour-and-
a-half driving distance from his parents,
Or else - if I disagree - I'm being accused of
cutting him off from his family
And forcing him into a life of isolation
One specific place and no leniency for what I want
- although I'm not even sure I have many wants,
They're not exactly described by a specific house in
a specific location
I want to be at peace in the here and now
I enjoy not being surrounded by people who are
like needy, angry, insecure, nagging parents
That refuse to walk the bitter path from self-doubt
and pain towards transparency and peace,
And instead choose to poke at me and pinch me in
order to reduce their self-induced painful
convulsions

Conscious Toxicity
Daria Hsu

People...
I love humans, but I despise people
With their unwillingness to give peace and love a chance,
To put down and burn their masks,
To throw social distancing to the curb
And just be brutally raw and courageously open to the possibility
Of everything being perfect, exactly as it needs to be in the here and now
No need to rush, to reprimand, to live in anger, fear, or any type of want,
Paradise is available to us here on Earth
Only if we are willing to take a step back and see it,
If we don't force and trust in magic
I feel it within myself but Michael, with his powerless, manless whining, ruins it
When he clearly accuses me of things his mom has hurt him with - not I,
Or when he pushes to live within a certain radius of his parents
That's when all his sex appeal is lost upon me
I do feel thirsty these days

Conscious Toxicity
Daria Hsu

But not for Michael's moping, moaning demands
to immediately escape the hardships we face in
Taipei (many of them in his own head)
For the immediate "alleviation" within a certain
radius of his parents' house -
That is the exact opposite of the man (or woman)
that I'm thirsty for these days
(Our) marriage is a ride: the highs are very high,
the lows are disturbing to our son
Needless to say, we're in a low if I am thirsting
after handsome blond manly movie actors,
Friendly young Asian guys who sold me sushi rolls
at a to-go window,
And mature spiritually-conscious women
He's been, he is my all - motherly-caring, loyally
present at my every beck and call,
Able to see what most couldn't even dream of
seeing,
But he can also be critical and moody and angry,
I fail to see the man in him these days
We haven't had sex in so long
We're focused (he's focused) on escaping Taiwan,
On moving to a house in California that we can
afford
It irks me and turns me off like crazy that he puts
an hour-and-a-half distance from his parents'

Conscious Toxicity
Daria Hsu

house as one of the main criteria - can't we be
adult and sufficient and move anywhere in
California and build a beautiful family and life?!
His parents in their own time moved from Taiwan
to Georgia, USA then to Northern California then
to Southern California without any regard to
where their own parents lived (Taiwan)
So Michael's constant nagging and pushing to live
within close driving distance of his father and
mother feels so non-masculine, off-putting...
Although at this point, maybe I'm just looking for
reasons to find him unattractive:
His red dots (allergy?) all over his belly and chest,
his lack of muscles, and his very angry, yelling,
aggressive demeanor (with Zen watching all of
that) when I suggest taking a break from the house
search or just living in the here and now in Taiwan
and not creating the urgency to escape like
refugees back to California, his lack of willingness
to consider anything outside of ninety minutes
from parents (although to be fair, he did look up
homes in Central California but then said it's too
hot and too polluted - yet when I pointed out the
pollution index for Crestline which was also quite
high he glanced past it as an "exception"...) -

Conscious Toxicity
Daria Hsu

Ah, I don't want to get weighed down by the miniature, insignificant details of our arguments, But his general pettiness over having his wishes met with disregard for mine, his unwillingness to listen to what I suggest or want, his volatile uncontrollable anger outbursts - gosh, all of that is so, so, so very off-putting, unsexy, and the opposite of masculine, or rather: mature

It feels like I'm surrounded by an old, argumentative hag who sells noodles at an outdoor market,

Because I can't stand being around him like that, and because he refuses to go out and have fun in parks or at beaches on most days (he demands his me-time, which I know he deserves - but he also is in a self-induced prison - to be fair, I force him into prison just like his mom did by manipulating and trying to dissuade him from leaving our home to run any errands - my biggest fear being Michael leaving and never returning home, I have my own demons in my closet...)

So that is how we live, with demons and all

Trying to survive

What can I say? Having a child takes away all the sexy that was there to begin with

Conscious Toxicity
Daria Hsu

It's labor, every day, non-ending, sometimes with
what my mom used to call "one's soul being pulled
out of one's body by the child"
We are in love; don't you question that
I love him
Zenny loves him
I'm just not attracted to him right now
But I also feel exhausted, like I need a soft place to
put my head down and relax from the zoo we've
been living through
Our home is a zoo
People are questionable creatures - there are some
bad apples, and some good
We'll make it through, darling, I know
We'll grow old together and have wild sex
Please, God, give us wild sex
More lovely children
And a beautiful safe haven of a home
Maybe we both just need to focus on what
matters? And the only thing that matters in times
of rockiness and upheaval is the here and now
One step at a time
Gosh, only to survive July
Actually, God: to learn to thrive this July
To feel our growing peace this July
That is what matters

Conscious Toxicity
Daria Hsu

Despite all the crap we're going through and how I
feel, my husband is a silent hero
He bought Zen food in scorching heat and now is
feeding, cleaning walls from mango smoothie that
Zen threw - while I write my poem
I think he is a keeper, girls
Bless him!
The way we filter water is by holding the water
filter above a teapot
You see, I accidentally broke the pitcher
And because the water filter is slippery against the
teapot's surface, when we put it on top to filter, it
often slips and the whole receptacle of water spills
all over the floor
More labor
Labor in love
In the ability to find peace and rest in moments
Eternity? The rest of life? I don't know what comes
But peace and quiet, relaxing moments of
contemplation are available to us in the here and
now if we dare stop for a bit
Hugs and kisses are available too
We desperately need those, dear

74.

Conscious Toxicity
Daria Hsu

I don't feel attracted to you anymore...
I don't! And every time your mother says
something typically
Intrusive and toxic towards our family,
And I call it out in indignation and you
Correct me that she is not a toxic person, just her
behavior is,
And then add that you want us to do monthly
weekend sleepovers
At your parents' house,
And that you don't mind your controlling,
possessive parents
Picking us up from LAX when we arrive,
Us sitting in the backseat like children,
Your dad driving nervously, horribly, but with
silent authority
That intimidates and stinks up the whole car,
While your helicopter mom talks shallow
sweetness and toxic nonsense to us
From the front passenger seat inside her luxurious
`imposing Lexus
As if we were kids in need of her constant
guidance,
Completely failing - no, refusing -

Conscious Toxicity
Daria Hsu

To accept her new role as grandmother and
mother of an adult, married man,
Your sex appeal shrinks like a wrinkly, tiny cock
You see, truth be told, it's not your lacking muscles
That deter me from desiring coitus -
You could be short and muscular,
Or tall and very thin,
Black, blond, Asian, woman, man, young, or old -
I'm well aware lust and love
Can creep up in different forms from different
corners -
It is your unresolved mommy and daddy issues
that irk me,
Your defensiveness when I call out their behavior
that simply has no place in our marriage,
Your unwavering willingness to keep returning to
their house and sleeping over there,
You viewing me and fighting me every day
through a lens that screams, "Mommy!!!"
L said a woman likes to be contained
How ridiculous, I thought at first,
But now I understand that's exactly what's missing
from our marriage
I feel served, pampered even, by your unwavering,
loyal, motherly-like actions and presence,
They make me appreciate you deeply,

Conscious Toxicity
Daria Hsu

But I do not feel contained by you at all
I feel like it is me - alone - next to you - alone - every day,
Our two worlds sometimes coexisting in the most joyful and elated way
And sometimes barely, in deepest frustration and pain
Sure, they overlap quite a bit, there are many points of contact,
But our worlds are not within each other, not intertwined from the ground up - roots and all -
I'm not within you and you are not within me
In a way we're yearlong friends who co-parent
Because that powerful, masculine oomph is missing from you,
And it drains and bleeds what could be the loveliest, hottest marriage
In a way it boils down to you continuously failing to fully claim, to stand in your full power -
The power that your parents stole from you in the sickest, most toxic way
And continue to do so with their seemingly harmless comments, texts, and even seeming actions of goodwill here and there and everywhere, enveloping you in complete disempowerment,

Conscious Toxicity
Daria Hsu

Cutting off your dick one inch at a time,
And me having to fight them against cutting off any more of what is left,
And newly also against cutting off Zen's dick little by little
Because your mom is already trying
That lady will chew off pieces of her own son and grandson without a slightest reservation,
All the while sweetly singing Chinese songs and giving compliments
While your dad tries to stop her but his awareness of what she does reaches only the tip of her iceberg
(Or maybe he's just exhausted from dealing with her in that way his whole life - who knows?)
And that's why, darling, I won't be getting picked up from LAX by your parents,
Nor doing monthly family sleepovers at your parents' house
I'd be truly ungrateful and blind to not acknowledge the long way you have come since I met you,
But you have ways to go for our marriage to stop bleeding
And while you walk those ways toward reclaiming your power,

Conscious Toxicity
Daria Hsu

I'll help along to keep your cock from being turned
into a pussy
Consider it a favor from your loving, sex-starved
wife

75.

I may not want to be here anymore
I may want to embark on our Czech travels and
our new-home-in-California adventure
I may crave the security of a closed and done real
estate deal,
But I know I need to practice my patience as I
linger in the unknown just a little bit longer,
And for all I know (I know!) I'll come to miss this
life in Taipei
They may be filled with sweat, hard work, and
jumping hurdles,
But they're also filled with love, our souls' lightness
and joy, our youth and our faith in a fun and
brighter future
They're filled with experiences that grow us, help
us grow closer to each other than before, mature
into fuller, more secure, and outspoken versions of
ourselves

Conscious Toxicity
Daria Hsu

I like the new us,
And for the first time in my life, as I am finding
towards a deeper, truer me,
I am beginning to enjoy sex,
A sexual me, ability to initiate and enjoy sex with
my partner,
To claim myself in our marriage as a sensuous
woman with sexual needs and desires and
fantasies...
Oh boy, does it feel good to claim that new me!
To be me, to speak me, to live me ~
To be us, to speak us, to live us ~
Without feeling the need for parental approval or
for prolonged explanations to strangers or friends
~
To be happy and live our lives no matter the
surrounding noise and reactions
We'll jump hurdles, we'll cultivate patience,
We'll face uncomfortable feelings that come up ~
All the while reclaiming ourselves: all those
beautiful precious pieces of ourselves that
somehow went missing over the course of our
childhoods and our previous lives

76.

Conscious Toxicity
Daria Hsu

Dreadful quiet,
Lonely sunshine,
Soul-wrenching silence -
Except for the occasional
Clitter-clatter of a passing tram,
No faces to be seen in windows,
Blinds tightly closed

I'd like to escape this depressing,
Post-boom feel of Prague -
It brings me too close to unpleasant childhood
feelings -
But I know I shouldn't try to escape
So, instead, I take a pen and a notepad,
And I write, sitting in this quiet,
As if waiting for something to happen:
Maybe a friendly face to knock on our door and
Welcome us to the neighborhood?
Or annoyingly loud crowds of
Tourists to pass by under our
Windows just like back in the
Good old - freer - times?

It feels like we live in a mostly
Abandoned building in the

Conscious Toxicity
Daria Hsu

Half-abandoned city center
Where, just two years ago,
I was complaining to Michael
About the crowds of tourists
Making it impossible to walk just a few steps
Now everybody left
Only we remain in this dreadful silence

77.

As I'm sitting by the window that is wide open into
the backyard,
I remember this exact scent
From my childhood and my youth that were spent
here
The gentle, mild, caressing wind,
Indistinct chatter from the neighboring windows -
To others it may seem welcoming and refreshing,
To some it may seem entertaining or mundane,
The old, stately buildings,
The majestic, generous tree of
Sprawling green leaves,
The insanely slowly passing clouds -
So slow, this enough
Could drive me to

Conscious Toxicity
Daria Hsu

A breakdown and despair,
The sunlight steadily streaming
Through the clouds at old
Residential buildings - I know its exact quality,
Its exact angle, its exact level of illumination -
I recognize all this too well -
While anywhere else they'd be
A perfect backdrop for peaceful
Contemplation - in this city[1],
In this country[2], in this part of the continent, they
cause me
Nothing but heartbreak,
Discomfort, alienation, a surprising lack of
Warmth and peace,
For God's sake! So many
Balconies, so many
Windows - but where
Are all the people?
Such dreadful cemetery-like quiet in the most
perfect sunshine - it lacks the soulfulness,
The soulfulness I desperately needed
As a child

[1] Prague
[2] Czech Republic

Conscious Toxicity
Daria Hsu

78.

Goodbye, Czech Republic, (Central) Europe,
goodbye!
You won't miss me,
And I know for sure: I won't miss you
You have repressed me in many different ways
That caused me to doubt my humanity and worth
You have been cynical and cruel,
Elitist Europe, a continent lacking soul
Like an old ho you are, that has seen it all and
nothing surprises her anymore
Your elaborately crafted buildings are icy cold to
me
There is no happiness, no joy streaming through
their windows
The many potentially gorgeous corners
Are populated by people who refuse
To see beyond the four prescribed
Walls of their average existence,
Who take repression with a pinch of salt,
Yet still as default
Foreigners and locals alike
Are jaded, not in a comforting way,
Ready to reprimand and

Conscious Toxicity
Daria Hsu

Become unpleasant - plain toxic! -
At every opportunity
Locals certainly bitch and whine about repression
And even project it onto innocent young children
Post factum, after others have spilled sweat and
Blood and tears to set them free,
But they do absolutely nothing to
Stand up, speak up in the moment,
To imagine in the moment something purer,
Lighter, freer for their
Children -
No, there is no future in this
Gray, cynical, mundane place for me.
A place that has lost all its
Childish dreaminess, innocence, and hope
A poem of hatred this may be,
But hatred breeds hatred…
You should know that like no one else, Europe
In short: I've had enough of you.
So goodbye, Czech Republic! Central Europe!
Adieu, L'Europe!

Нам не по пути.[1]

---

[1] We are on different paths.

Conscious Toxicity
Daria Hsu

79.

Something's cooking,
I can smell it in the air
In this clean, beautiful apartment,
Surrounded by stately old buildings,
Walking freely, breathing freely -
What cause is there for me to doubt?
And yet I feel deeply uncomfortable
As if in anticipation of something bigger,
Of greater evil to come
It's scary, to be plain honest,
To have so many people close to us (back in the
US) completely lost to darkness and pain
It almost feels like we're about
To move into the eyes of this
Devilish hurricane
Where friends and family
Have merged with the "medical" evil
Zombies, pawns, they are not people,
They're something else with human faces,
They're disconnected from their souls, their higher
selves -
They've desecrated their bodies,
Their beautiful bodies that God so
Lovingly gifted them at birth

Conscious Toxicity
Daria Hsu

I'm beginning to appreciate Czech people
They may not be protesting in outright revolts and
revolutions,
But many of them see through this craziness
And I have witnessed quiet, peaceful, crucial
Non-compliance among them
I know they'll come out of this -
Maybe not unscathed, none of us will come
Out unscathed - but having kept their souls,
Which brings me peace
They know that this is all
A game, and as long as they
Appear to go along with this madness,
They will keep living more or less
The same: not perfectly, not heroically,
Czech people certainly have issues, and yet
There's wisdom in the way they are
For me, I know I'm meant to go
Where darkness has set in and
Channel all my power to light
Up that forsaken corner of earth:
California, USA
It's scary, I know not what's to come,
How will we survive if they cut us
Off from food,
How will we raise our child,

Conscious Toxicity
Daria Hsu

Grow our family bigger,
Provide an education, a sense of normalcy
Where devil is slowly but surely
Taking possession?
And yet, I can't afford to be afraid
To end this evil madness, I must
Face it where it rages wild
Again, we will rejoice someday
In freedom - freedom for all,
With a deeper connection with ourselves
And other humans, animals, and
Plants
Light shall prevail
Light will prevail!
Yes! Light prevails

80.

I'm sick, a sore throat, tired,
Exhausted, achy head,
Constantly running nose,
The skin under my nose has started to hurt,
Even my ears are getting clogged
I hate it here
I feel uncomfortable in my body,

Conscious Toxicity
Daria Hsu

A bit feverish
In this country that makes me feel uncomfortably
self-aware, small, quiet-mouthed
I keep thinking of Western Europe... France,
England, Italy...
Anywhere would be better... not as
claustrophobic,
I wouldn't have to conform
Of course, in truth, what do I know
What it's like to live in those places - I've only
visited them,
And yet visions of Africans and Arabs come up,
Who are now French,
I remember seeing many of them on the Paris train
Visions of Indians come up, who are now British
Indian food seemed to have become part of British
national fare when we visited long time ago
Despite the many issues that those countries have -
I do feel that there is more of a sense of acceptance
Of immigrants-turned-locals there,
At least there exist descriptions that acknowledge
them:
French Arab, British Indian
Having grown up here since eight years old,
I can't even claim that description: Czech
Russian...

Conscious Toxicity
Daria Hsu

They'd laugh at me!
Sure, I can say that I'm Czech Russian but I'll never
be one of the Czechs -
The way Eliskas, Jitkas, and Bozenkas are
I'll forever be (unspokenly, maybe) THAT Russian
girl
Who grew up in Czech Republic
In order to belong here,
In order to be home here,
I'd have to castrate myself,
To speak Czech with a perfect accent,
To deny my place of birth (which
I'm disconnected from, but
Which nevertheless is real),
I'd have to be a carbon copy of them:
Polite, unfriendly, not emotional, down to earth,
Jaded, cliquey, cynical, trigger-happy,
Knowledgeable about ordering beer,
I'd have to have a Czech heart
(What is the secret to the Czech heart?)
To be one of them
Dissent is not welcome
Neither is it in Taiwan, of course
I know these are just labels, and
It is possible to feel unwelcome, not at home in
many other countries,

Conscious Toxicity
Daria Hsu

But I grew up here,
I suffered here - so for me,
This place is soured with the taste of my tears
My suffering here matters
It was not in vain
Of course, it's mixed with bitterness, a vengeful
Wish to blast them for having hurt me when I was
At my weakest, most unprotected, just a child,
Yet I may as well feel bitter and spiteful at the
whole human race,
My honey says, and he is right
For I have witnessed the same close-mindedness,
same lack of human love
In the Taiwanese, and Russians,
And Americans -
It is a worldwide problem that manifests and hurts
on very local levels
And yet this particular flavor -
Post-communist one - is particularly well-known
to me: it
Shows up most in the service industry -
Unfriendly, plain rude,
And ready to talk back at you with no fear of
repercussions -
If you don't like being treated like a dog -
Go to a different store where they will

Conscious Toxicity
Daria Hsu

Treat you like a pig
Ah, these human-made systems have done
So much damage to us, humans:
Both eastern bloc Communism and western
Capitalism
Because in the end no system will work
If it is not based on honest awareness,
Love, and acceptance of ourselves and others:
Humans, animals, and plants
Systems based on human pain,
Interpreted through the lens of pain, will only
Breed pain for everyone on Mother Earth

81.

And what if we never, ever, ever end up leaving here,
If this is all a test and we are failing,
If Berlin Wall ends up closing down on us and we end up on the wrong side of it?
I'm growing scared to the point where my ego, my superficial wishes, my fears, my insecurities become so small in contrast to the magnitude of it all
I keep speaking English to Zen

Conscious Toxicity
Daria Hsu

We all speak English to each other in a non-English-speaking country
It feels more familiar and chill in a cool, reserved, edgy, restrictive environment
But my fear remains that we will always be stuck here, the little American island banned from our return to the US
What a sad prospect!
Until we finalize our house purchase, I am stuck between feeling stuck in Michael's parents' house and feeling stuck in the Czech Republic, both places haunted, heavy, traumatized
To be stuck between a rock and a hard place with no clear deadline of being set free
Is quite terrifying,
Even though I know it's all in my head, within me,
And thus within me I shall find my freedom again
I'm afraid of Michael's parents' overwhelming, intrusive energy with toxic undertones... but I can be more mature than that,
And stronger
I'm afraid of forever being stuck in the Czech Republic, resolving myself to a life in this small green country that never quite feels like home -
Which of these two fears is bigger, I wonder

Conscious Toxicity
Daria Hsu

They both loom large over my head and make me
feel like I am sinking deep

82.

Hey girl,
There are many ways to be sexual,
And all of them are good
You and your body have been
Through a lot,
And you survived!
That alone is cause for celebration
You are not your needy parents'
Comfort blanket,
Nor your husband's
Tool for satisfaction
So you go and get all
The orgasms you can because
You deserve them:
With your husband or…
Imagination!
You are not a consolation prize
Your body is fire!
Your sexy butt curves
So nicely in those blue panties

Conscious Toxicity
Daria Hsu

As you put on your dress
You don't need anyone's approval
(Nor help) to know the heights of
Pleasure
And if there is anything to regret at all,
Regret the days you did not
Love your body
Because each day is precious,
And your body is gold
You are your own happiness's
Cause and effect
So go get those orgasms, girl!
You are so worth it

83.

Oh-oh
I spot oppression in my own
Husband
And my brother
Every time my husband
Gives me a hard time
On my own fucking
Thirty-first birthday
Over my short hair,

Conscious Toxicity
Daria Hsu

Over the restaurants I choose to
Ring in the new
Decade,
My husband and my brother
Giving me a hard time over my dress,
My brother gently suggesting that I mask up,
My husband giving me a hard
Time over money
When ordering my birthday meal
They are both products of
Their mothers, they are victims of their mothers:
Repressive mothers breed
Repressive sons
It really hurts to see
The same repression
That hurt me in my parents and in society
In my own brother and my own husband…
But we easily become our parents,
Reenacting centuries of repressive,
Sick, castrating pain
Despite criticizing
Our parents, calling them
Out, hurting because of
How they hurt us
When I saw my brother
Yesterday for the first time

Conscious Toxicity
Daria Hsu

In eight or nine months...
Tall, slim, in a respirator,
Standing alone in the middle of the mall...
I first saw...
My father! He looked
Like a copy of my father!
When we started talking,
I recognized my brother in him...
But I also recognized
My mother's pain in him,
Like I recognize
My mother-in-law's pain
In my own husband
Mothers... you do so much more
Than birth future men...
You mold them into future men
Every time you reclaim
Your lost or broken parts,
You heal your broken spirit and body that's half-
asleep,
Every time you rejoice in life
You mold the future generation
So women, liberate yourselves!
Your liberation is mankind's
Liberation.

Conscious Toxicity
Daria Hsu

84.

People...
Are full of Insecurities
And pain
They often make little sense, those illogical creatures,
Like robots, they relive and cause - over and over again - the same pain to themselves and others

People...
Are full of pain, anxiety, and crazy, quirky complexes
Controlled by egos - some more so than others
They constantly misunderstand each other and feel misunderstood due to the barrier of their own past traumas that they choose to keep reliving in their present
They project their own parents (the non-fun, hurtful, sick, and twisted parts of parents) onto each other, from which an extraordinary, sometimes deadly mess results that rubs so much unnecessary salt into already bleeding wounds

But...

Conscious Toxicity
Daria Hsu

Within their robotic, traumatized existence, people
ARE capable of glimpses of love
Their love is often limited to specific people and
specific situations
It has its own bounds and rules

But in some people...
That love extends widely, patiently, sacrificially
into the unknown, into the painful, and we call
those people "Jesus," "Buddha," "righteous among
the nations," "hero," "dad," "grandpa", "auntie,"
"teacher," "neighbor," "college friend"
Those people are human
Upon them our humanity rests, survives, and has a
hope of thriving

People...
I dislike them
I feel contempt for them
I feel alienated from those creatures
No matter how long or well you believe to know
them, they repeatedly disappoint and disillusion
and break hearts

But humans...
Oh, I love them!

Conscious Toxicity
Daria Hsu

With all my heart

I wish there were more humans on this Earth

85.

A failed investment:
A nauseated feeling in my stomach,
Not hungry, tears in my eyes,
I failed my family
Now that life is finally real...
A blow!
We just took out a mortgage AND a car loan,
A beautiful new house and car,
A toddler,
Now that every dollar matters,
With astronomic food and gas expenses too
And toys and household items to be purchased...
Did it have to happen now? NOW?
As we are starting our new life,
Finally, after years of struggling...
Success feels good, feels stable, new, yet always,
always busy
But suddenly a setback
Ah, it seems like it will never end...

Conscious Toxicity
Daria Hsu

But the good thing is that it reminds me to treasure
all that was so painfully, painstakingly achieved,
To treasure and protect my values above all
I should not forget that I have them for a reason
And that they will not be given up for a superficial
afternoon lunch at a Chinese restaurant with
people gone mad,
I should not forget to insure my profits instead of
gambling in mindless, aimless hopes of more and
more -
After all the struggles, painful setbacks, seemingly
never-ending lows, I know better than that
I don't need to waste my precious life on people
and activities that don't align with lessons so hard-
learned

86.

My heart is broken over ... Money
I thought I was over it:
Money is superficial, so toxic, so American,
And yet here I am facing a prospect of losing a few
thousand and
I am decomposing.
The biggest pain is that of having disappointed:

Conscious Toxicity
Daria Hsu

I know how much he fears and hopes for every
hard-earned hundred-plus dollars,
The burden of a mortgage, a car loan, daily
expenses lying heavy on his shoulders,
The deeper-seated painful fear of not being able to
provide for his family always haunting him
I was so happy at the prospect of relieving him of
that constant pain,
Of helping my family gain comfort, stability, and
footing in this country,
And now I made us worse off instead
I am terrified of telling him about this
He will flip out
He will prevent me from investing in the future
And yet I - the expansive, naive optimist when it
comes to making money -
Do still believe that I can somehow make this
money back
And then some, more, more, more!
Day trading is the sweetest gamble, most addictive,
When my profits grow, it is an inexplicable high
I don't quite understand: what went wrong this
time?
My ego is addicted to doing it at all costs
I need to be reminded in the midst of recurring
successes

Conscious Toxicity
Daria Hsu

That I am only human, a human gambler
I don't know how to tell him
I won't tell him
I will try one more time
It will be my last: I will either win big or I will lose
it all
It is quite terrifying
But do I have a choice?
To admit my failure would mean days, weeks of
being
Restrained and reprimanded
While I know deep inside that I can make it work
The responsibility is huge
It terrifies me
I feel like all of my family's livelihood is at stake
It is: after all, he was beginning to count on my
weekly profits to pay bills
And now... Where did I go wrong?
How can I make it right?
I must, I will make it right again

87.

Some days are harder,
Some are easier,

Conscious Toxicity
Daria Hsu

Today is painful
As much as it hurts to be banned from a family wedding over our vaccine status,
It hurts even more to watch my husband be unwilling to set a clear boundary with this toxicity,
Allowing those who wined and dined gladly and eagerly at our own wedding
To nonchalantly exclude us from theirs,
Unwilling to tell them, wait, NO! You don't get to treat me and my wife and son like this
It is sickening that my husband's own parents not only don't speak up in support of us
But quietly follow along with this evil and gladly go to the wedding and celebrate
While their own son and grandson have been banned!
Ironically, these people are very sick despite trying to avoid sickness in the most ridiculous ways
As wrong as vaccine mandates are in job and university settings,
They are most atrocious when created and enforced by people who claim to love you

88.

Conscious Toxicity
Daria Hsu

You don't get to tamper with my good, kind heart
No, you don't
I am a good girl
I am a kind girl
You don't get to tamper with my heart or my son's heart
You don't get to ban me from a wedding and act like nothing happened
You don't get to march along to evil that's directly affecting my son and tell me to respect your choice to do so
You don't get to tell me to be quiet when I speak up against this sickness in your family and divert the conversation to how sick I am
You don't
If only I listen to my heart, I know what's right and what's wrong
And there's no reason in the world for me to hush hush like your family does about toxicity.
I'll speak up and raise all hell if it is for a good cause
I'll make you uncomfortable and edgy in your seat
It's your free will to perpetuate and perpetrate toxicity
And it's mine to speak up

Conscious Toxicity
Daria Hsu

89.

I feel lonely,
Completely, utterly alone
I look at those people: they have siblings, cousins, parents, grandmas, children, nephews, nieces, friends...
They live in beautiful houses in San Francisco
While I live on a dry, lonely mountain in smogged-up Southern California,
In desert air, where plants are dry, dry, dry
The air is so dry here it's impossible to live without a humidifier,
In isolation from relationships with family and friends (I said goodbye to the remaining ones),
In isolation on a mountain at 8000 feet -
It hurts so much to be vaccine mandated out of their wedding while still being asked to sustain a relationship with them
It hurts to have them in my life -
They seem abundant, happy, and connected to each other,
All agreeing, all in tune -
While I disagree, alone, it almost feels like I can't take it

Conscious Toxicity
Daria Hsu

Every time I see them, I inevitably compare
And I inevitable lose,
Because I don't live in San Francisco,
And I don't have three close siblings in the same city,
As well as cousins, aunts and friends
I've wished so many times to be like them, to be them, to be part of them,
But this vaccine mandated exclusion is a stark reminder that I am not,
So then I will walk my path
I don't want to associate with them,
And yet my husband wants to keep the relationship that causes me so much pain
With people that exhibited the opposite of love with their choice
And it hurts, terrifies me frankly that my husband is going along with this toxicity,
Suddenly failing to see the perversity of vaccine mandates within family

90.

Don't push me onto them,
And you will have your peace

Conscious Toxicity
Daria Hsu

Your family is a bunch of toxic psychos
Just because they have fancier clothes, and cars,
and houses than mine
Does not make them any less sick
Mandating vaccine passports and
Not speaking up about it as if everything were
normal
Is sick and not along my life path
The fact that I speak up against this
And your dad ignores me is sick and toxic,
You are now using the same faulty logic your dad
and mom and all those sickos use: free will, THEIR
wedding
Free will does not equal doing anything, anytime,
anywhere
By that account murder is OK because it is free will
Excluding family members from a wedding
because they don't want to get a new vaccine with
unknown side effects is wrong, the opposite of love
that you claim to share with those said family
members that excluded you from their wedding,
that treat you like a doormat - which you are
seemingly OK with,
You take out all your pent up anger and irritation
on me
Our family suffers because of this!

Conscious Toxicity
Daria Hsu

It's sickening to watch you suddenly flip in almost support and certainly tolerance of this nasty sick shit,
Because "family,"
Because "love"
Where was that family when they were happily dancing their night away at the wedding yesterday?
Where was that love when they all conveniently avoided mentioning that we were not on the invitation for their wedding,
Even though they were all guests of honor at our wedding?
Fuck this sick shit!
You pushed me to associate with them once -
No more
They'll need to change to deserve to be part of my and our son's life
If you want to be a doormat or support medical fascism that's being enforced onto our family, you're on your own

91.

I am a nobody to them

Conscious Toxicity
Daria Hsu

They have a good life without me
They don't even think about me
They couldn't care less how I or we will react if
they ban us from their wedding,
They just go ahead and do it
I thought I was someone to them,
I so badly wanted to be like them:
A big family, beautiful houses and cars,
Living in a beautiful city,
Lots of relatives, friends.
They all have each other,
A close-knit family clan,
I have none of that. None!
Maybe they care about my husband
To a degree, not as much as about each other
Since they invited each other but not him,
But I... I am a nobody to them,
And I can't even say I matter to my friends
anymore
I stopped responding and no one came rushing,
Inquiring after me, asking what's wrong.
I feel like I have a good, kind heart
I have always cared about my friends
I have always wanted to be on good terms with
Michael's cousins, family,

Conscious Toxicity
Daria Hsu

But why is it that none of these people care about
me,
Love me,
Hear me,
Understand me?
No, they just live their lives and seemingly couldn't
care less about me or what I have to say
My own husband couldn't care less at this point
He just holds on to his relationship with them,
People who I don't resonate with,
Who don't care about me at all!!!
Oh, how it hurts
To see their huge family
Who seemingly love each other and get along and
celebrate together,
Who go way back in history
I don't have that
Who cares about me?
Who do I go way back with?
My son
My dearest, sweetest son
My loveliest ray of sunshine
I feel so bad crying in front of him, around him,
Not being the joyful content mother he deserves,
Breaking his heart with my feelings of loneliness,
Of exclusion from the world

Conscious Toxicity
Daria Hsu

But neither can I force myself to be part of
something that doesn't feel like it builds me up,
Supports me,
Brings me lasting joy and peace
Am I doing something very wrong
By excluding myself from the world
From almost all people I have known?
Will I die all alone and lonely
Because of my actions?
Or do I need to retreat from people,
From the world, in order to gain a deeper
understanding,
To find a more direct path to myself?
I don't want to be intertwined in their masks
And vaccine passports, in their crazy

92.

- 911, what's your emergency?
- Hi! Our son is missing! He is two years old! We came to the awards ceremony and we were in a rush because we were late. We are always in a rush. We parked in the underground garage and rushed out of the car. I asked my husband to get our son so he did and he raced ahead to the

Conscious Toxicity
Daria Hsu

concert hall as I walked behind. I lost them out of sight. When I arrived at the concert hall and saw my husband again, everything was so busy because we had to register at the entry that I got distracted and didn't notice our son was missing. Also, his grandparents came with us so I guess I naturally assumed he would be with his grandparents while we registered. But after we did, I suddenly realized our son was missing so I asked my husband, "Where is Zen?!" and that's when we realized he wasn't in the concert hall! We ran out into the street. I ran across the bridge back towards the parking garage yelling, "Zenny! Zenny!" but I can't find him. He is only two years old and even if he hears his name he won't necessarily know to respond back or walk towards me. I can't see him anywhere! Now I am back in the garage but he isn't here either! Please help me! He is only two years old! We were in such a rush, we completely lost track of him.

I always wanted a different life: richer, bigger house, more children, San Francisco, Cinque Terre, Malibu, Santa Barbara.

But now that I suddenly lost it all, all I want is my old life back! Gone suddenly, in an instant, while I was busy looking the other way, busy being busy.

Conscious Toxicity
Daria Hsu

Zenny! My child! My beloved, dear baby! Where are you?!

93.

Oh… how it hurts…
Oh… how it hurts…
To be treated so unlovingly,
With so much disdain,
Because you are completely, utterly lost
In your pain, in your delusional perception of me
as your narcissistic mother
She did the harm, yet I take the brunt of her
actions every day,
And so does our son,
You attacking me, accusing me,
Ah, these endless, endless accusations
I breathe - and you accuse me
Oh dear, you've turned into a monster
Oh my, how much it hurts to not be given an
ounce of love by you
No, no! Resentment and accusations are all I'm
worthy of in your crazed eyes
Oh, it hurts to be treated so by you,

Conscious Toxicity
Daria Hsu

The father of my son, my boyfriend, fiancé, lover, husband
How much of this can I take? Should I take?
Our son is the decisive part of this equation,
His well-being is the answer to my questions
He needs a father, yes, of course, he needs a father,
But he should not be witnessing his father verbally attacking,
Harassing, controlling his mom,
His father being egged on, spellbound
By some questionable Instagram healer from Romania
Whom he has placed on a pedestal and to whom he out of the blue
Reveals the most intimate details of our marriage and family life
Oh gods! I call upon you! What is going on?
Who is this healer woman who has latched onto our family,
Offering my husband free healing sessions,
Craftily showering him with big fancy words of healing, regression, and shadow work?
What is she giving him that I have failed to give?
Where was I too distracted, too self-preoccupied, too ego-based,
Too carried away with the business of life,

Conscious Toxicity
Daria Hsu

That she succeeded in entering our marriage and
prying, hypnotizing,
Shaking up, and stabbing our marriage from
oceans away?
I can't confide in my own husband anymore,
Because he reports back to her anything I do or say
And she tells him not to tell me what she tells him
Michael, what happened? How can you be so lost
in your own pain
That you are slutting away the sacredness of our
marriage in the fake name of healing?
And how much of your fucked behavior should I
take?

94.

Ever since moving into this house,
It has been a non-stop struggle:
From the dead mouse in our bathtub
Through Michael talking to some dubious shadow
worker from Romania
Who can't stop messaging him pseudo-
psychological advice, a lot of it delusional talk
about how I am a manipulative narcissist to be
watched out for (get a life, lady),

Conscious Toxicity
Daria Hsu

To a high tax bill and a missed call on some issue with our investments
My body feels exhausted, weak as if I were ill,
The drama with Michael is devastating me: the yelling, accusations, threats of divorce, the Romanian witch egging Michael on to preserve his skewed image of me as a narcissist and planting sick ideas into his mind about me not wanting to work on myself, telling him to keep what she messages him about me a secret because I supposedly can't take it, messaging him even after Michael suggested taking a break from sessions and messaging for now
(I am floored that someone in the field of healing shadow work can have such a huge ego and be so delusional
She seems really hurt and slighted that I refused to get any more counselling with her and left her a negative review after reading the crap she sent to Michael about me while telling him to keep it a secret)
At the expense of karma coming after my ass immediately after I write this and killing off my beloved husband and son in some gruesome car accident,
I admit: I feel tired of this life

Conscious Toxicity
Daria Hsu

I want to get out of it
Finding mouse shit in the kitchen cabinet where
we store all our pots for cooking - after having
spent the whole day cleaning out mouse shit from
our home, sealing holes and watching Michael
turn into a monster over me having sealed too
many holes without having asked his opinion since
this is OUR house - is the last straw
Shit around our cooking dishes
I am disgusted
Yes, I wanted a house, but not one with mice
shitting inside
Yes, I wanted a house, but not with my husband
yelling, refusing my love,
Refusing to hear out my truth, instead putting on a
pedestal the truths of some Romanian witch he
found on Instagram a few weeks ago
Yes, I feel hurt and betrayed that he was willing to
give up on his love and trust for me so easily, the
moment someone came into his life and started
validating the heck out of him
That's all it took
You live with someone, are married to someone,
have a child with someone,

Conscious Toxicity
Daria Hsu

And yet - how well do you really know them? How well do you really know what's going through their head?
The most romantic thing about marriage is the wedding
Marriage is no romance
No sleeping, no cuddling in the same bed
No sex
No hugs, caresses, kisses
It's coexisting under the same roof, doing things for each other and for the family,
And trying not to end up in the divorce court as ancestral and childhood shit from both sides of our family floods is flooding us
That's not to say there is no light:
There is!
Despite defending her and telling me he has the right to continue his sessions with her,
He came to understand how his communication with her feels like it is betraying and desecrating our marriage
She keeps reaching out, but he has not messaged her back (for now, at least)
I appreciate that
And those moments, hours, days that Michael, Zen and I spend together, when we have the time of

Conscious Toxicity
Daria Hsu

our lives, laugh, have a blast, Michael being the
most loving, goofy father, Michael telling me
sweetly, quietly, "Love you too, honey" (so many
times he doesn't) - but the times he does, I
appreciate them
There are some great, great highs we have
And great lows that we fall into, from which we -
hopefully - recover
But will our son recover, having witnessed all of
this?

95.

Disgusting
Insufferable
Makes me want to get drunk on wine
(I took out a bottle and poured
But I know I shouldn't drink my feelings away)
Make me shiver in horror:
I want to jump into a hot shower
And wash off this sickening mess
I can't concentrate on my favorite book about
Pompeii
My thoughts keep drifting back

Conscious Toxicity
Daria Hsu

To the two Russian ladies we met at the
playground today
The heavier built one was especially outspoken
about
Getting her third vaccine
And showing an understanding for vaccine
mandates
Excusing her actions with fear of illness
And wanting to attend the symphony!
It made her and her friend's souls rejoice
To attend the symphony in their town, she said
So they kept getting injected to be allowed into
Events and locations denied to the unvaccinated
and untested
I spoke my truth but way too cautiously
Too softly maybe? I feel disappointed that I did not
shout
From the rooftops how disgusting this is
But we have few friends and I really want Zen
To play with other children so I was cautiously
honest
Now in retrospect, I shiver
Why did I text them to keep in touch?
Why was I so excited when they suggested to meet
up again?

Conscious Toxicity
Daria Hsu

Sickening, nauseating that people are willing to
sell their souls and bodies
For a concert or a symphony
Frightening, appalling that the children with
whom my son is playing
Are being raised by mothers who are in complete
peace
That my son is banned from society if he remains
uninjected
Then there's the Australian lady:
She told me
She'll beg and do anything for her son to get a fake
vaccine passport
So that he can go to school
To the school that only welcomes experimental
rabbits
To the school that bans children from talking
during lunch breaks
Why would you beg for that?
I'll never understand
People who are completely at peace with what's
going on
As long as they get their share of the cake,
As long as they get their seat at the fascist table
Disgust me

Conscious Toxicity
Daria Hsu

96.

Finally I have everything I ever wanted:
Four children... five!
A mansion in a gorgeous southern California
Neighborhood... with ocean views!
And a Victorian in San Francisco too
Everything to satisfy my ego!
I've checked off all the boxes on my bucket list
I've won, surprised, surpassed,
Perplexed, made proud and jealous
These past few decades have been success-studded
And brighter than the sun itself,
Yet somehow as I look back
These years seem empty and soulless
And I can't find that sweetness between me
And my husband anymore:
That sweetness, warmth, pure love
We used to share
Having achieved my ego's dream,
I've lost my heart's dream with my honey

97.

Conscious Toxicity
Daria Hsu

You are not coming back,
That makes me very sad.
The dreams I had of Sunday girls' brunches,
Of friends' picnics on the pacific coast,
Of fun celebrations and outings
Are not going to materialize
Let's celebrate what we still have:
An occasional video call…
Chat, banter, catch up, laughter, reminiscing
About the past…
And the goings on in our separate lives
That we have separately built for ourselves
And whose rewards and karmas we are now
Separately reaping
So much seeming history together,
I thought our heartfelt friendship
By the ocean waves would last forever
Like the California sun,
But you seem comfortable saying goodbye
For another month or few,
And I act like I am comfortable too

98.

Nauseous is how I feel

Conscious Toxicity
Daria Hsu

This much pain and trauma is
Too
Damn
Overwhelming
Much
There is a passed soul sitting in my passenger seat
talking to me
My mom is tearing out her hair in despair of grief
I'm taking to her silently, from thousands of miles
away
I'm going insane
I'm holding in the vomit
So desperately hoping it doesn't come out
I don't want to think about whether it would look
like a darkness of cockroaches if it were to come
out
Horror movie style

As a seven-year-old girl, I got food poisoning
From mushroom pizza
In nineteen nineties' Yeltsin's Russia
I was sick for weeks if not months
I was so weak I remember lying on my brother's
couch
Matter of factly coming to terms with the idea that
I was gonna die

Conscious Toxicity
Daria Hsu

And that was AFTER I started reconvalescing

I feel panicky
I fear I'm being abducted by aliens
I suspect I may be a medium like Long Island
Medium
I suspect I'm going crazy,
Completely asinine

99.

What kinda fucking healing can one get
When one feels one needs to heal
From life itself
From all of one's childhood
From that era, that time, that place
All those people in my childhood, how did they live,
Raise their children, attend weddings
While I was feeling so lonely and traumatized
Sitting by myself on the couch in my bedroom
Hearing my dad yelling at my mom
(Or at his pain?)
In the neighboring living room,
Hearing the quiet of my mom,
Not a healthy peaceful quiet,

Conscious Toxicity
Daria Hsu

A reserved passive aggressive quiet
Of a person in a bottomless pit of pain

And now decades later,
I and Michael yelling at each other
In front of Zen and Gaia
So heartbreaking for our children to witness this
I used to think it is so easy to raise children
In a joyful, non-traumatizing environment
Until I had them

100.

You have seen something that cannot be unseen
You've witnessed the line between life and death:
All it takes is one step back at the wrong time on
the wrong road
Yet a split second later
You gather yourself and go on to sing to your kids
And offer snacks and bubbles and sand toys
So desperately wanting to avoid their trauma
Telling them it's OK to feel scared
Trying to comfort them
Holding your terrified friend's hand and coaching
her through it

Conscious Toxicity
Daria Hsu

Watching out for your shell-shocked husband
You try to laugh extra hard in the immediate aftermath
You ask for no conversations on the way back
Just concentrate on driving please
You tell your husband
You want to concentrate on your friend's life problems
It helps you avoid facing your own painful mountain that you're trying to ignore
You look around and the first word
You see on the freeway billboards is DIE
In all caps, that's right
Now you're terrified
Is it destiny for him to graduate to heaven?
Is an evil presence, Jack the ripper, set on getting us no matter what?
Is the place this happened haunted or are we?
You briefly snooze off and wake up from a nightmare of bright lights about to crash into you
You consider driving only local streets from now on
The freeway seems like the most ominous place
With evil spirits behind cars out there to get you
You decide you'll never sleep or snooze
Always stay vigilant and alert

Conscious Toxicity
Daria Hsu

You pray and pray out loud to give the kids some semblance of peace
To try to find some meaning behind what just happened
But you know very well that on the inside you feel terror
As your husband parks the car and kisses your daughter sweetly sleeping in your arms
You lean towards his head and surreptitiously dip your nose into his hair
Breathing in its scent
You realize you have forgotten the smell of his hair
He doesn't want your to remember it
And so you suck it up and wonder if it is your marriage that is dead
At home as you come and tell him your usual gratitude and blessings for him in light of what happened
And he does not respond with the slightest sign of affection
You wonder how strongly you should be holding onto something that is no longer working:
Until you kill him out of your fear of facing loneliness and grief?
Or maybe you should let him go and he'll survive?

Conscious Toxicity
Daria Hsu

You're angry broken strangers living under the
same roof
Do you love him or the idea of loving him?
If you no longer remember the smell of his hair
If he doesn't want you to smell his hair
If all he sees is fat and failures
Then what is left?
You are too self-preoccupied, depressed and
anxious to tell
And now you're hiding in your bathroom
Your face buried in your hands
In silent terror
Sobbing

101.

You should be embarrassed of yourself
I feel very embarrassed
And I repress it
I try not to think about that message
I sent to my father-in-law
He is the sweetest, most caring grandpa
It's OK to call out grandma once in a while for
acting crazy
But with grandpa, the stoic emperor,

Conscious Toxicity
Daria Hsu

The reasonable provider who has done and
continues to do so much for us
Including paying for our lavish wedding,
Who loves our children dearly and treats them
patiently and respectfully,
With whom I'm on good terms
(with grandma too…),
I feel awkward to call him out,
To criticize the one that in my eyes is untouchable,
Seemingly elevated above us all,
His restraint from talking too much if at all
coupled with his history of choices appear to point
to his wisdom
So how can I dare to speak out?
He will likely remain silent but look down upon
me behind my back,
Thinking that I lack maturity or consciousness
How can I compete with someone older than my
parents in matters of wisdom and understanding?
In the grand scheme of life, I am a newborn,
Yelling, screaming, pouting, demanding, scared as
fuck,
Just barely starting to wake up from my newborn
slumber

Conscious Toxicity
Daria Hsu

And to - sort of - be able to differentiate between
mostly indistinct shapes and colors held up to my
face
My world consisting mostly of gray shadows in the
distance
That I observe semi-consciously in the brief time
gaps when I'm not fully preoccupied with my own
needs
He must think I'm embarrassingly crazy and
unrestrained like an angry stray dog, barking out
at everyone who has slighted me,
Or maybe he thinks I'm like a helpless sad puppy
trying to act strong and tough
Because in reality I am embarrassed, scared and
cold!

102.

Send help my way!
I won't take pills
No to ashwaghanda!
Not because there is anything wrong with
ashwaghanda
But because I want to get to the bottom of this pit
I want to keep falling falling falling

Conscious Toxicity
Daria Hsu

Until I finally reach the bottom
And make a new realization,
An epiphany!
I finally slept enough
Yet woke up more depressed than ever
Resting in bed made me realize just how depressed
I am
It's easy to distract myself with two little children
But they won't be little forever
And they will soak up my depression and grow up
depressed like me
So no ashwaghanda for me today
I feel this pain throughout my body
Flowing through my veins
In front of me is all I ever wanted
My dreams came true
The paradise I hadn't dared to dream would
manifest one day
Has manifested
Depression, though, hasn't lifted
Our fairytale wedding, rose gardens, the beaches
of Hawaii, travels across the world, travels near
and far, houses, expensive meals, an ever present
helpful devoted handsome wise husband, two
beautiful kids, a boy and a girl, close in age, our

Conscious Toxicity
Daria Hsu

own living space in California, nothing, NOTHING
has solved it
Ashwaghanda provides temporary relief
But how authentic is peace derived from pills, even
if they're herbs?
And so I suspect a deeper peace may come from
acknowledging that the world can be a brutal
place:
Husbands and children get killed in hit and runs,
the world goes on
People get scarred by war,
Yet new families are started,
Children grow up with heavily depressed,
combative, non-present parents
But does anyone batter an eye?
The Earth keeps revolving around its axis!
But instead of repressing the horrible and
unacceptable that has happened or could happen,
Why not openly acknowledge it as a reality
And contribute something healing to the world
Like ashwaghanda does?

103.

I beg you to come back

Conscious Toxicity
Daria Hsu

On my knees I beg you
Please don't leave me
Please love me, I beg you
Don't leave the emptiness you left behind after you
left unfilled
Where are you
I cannot go on without you
I did load up on ashwaghanda
But that doesn't mend a broken heart
You stopped giving me kisses, hugging me
You pushed away my every hug
You yelled
I ignored, didn't talk to you
I miss you
How can I go on without you
I don't want another man
I want you
Your loving self
The one that would never leave
I left my mother and stopped talking to her
And now you left me
I wonder is it karma
Now that you left I remember
You used to say life with me is full of torture
That's why I left my mother
Life with her was full of suffering

Conscious Toxicity
Daria Hsu

I miss you, I love you
Where are you
Where are you
Where is my husband
You deleted my on Facebook as your friend
So I blocked your Facebook and emails
I'm too proud to reach out
But also don't want to go back to the same
arguments and yelling, lack of affection and of
physical touch and criticism
But now that you're gone I try to replicate what
you used to do:
No sugary juice, almond milk instead for our kids...
My heart is breaking into a thousand pieces
I'm worried whether you feel better without me
I don't feel better without you
How can I keep staying in this apartment when
your bedroom is empty
Why did you never let me sleep in your bed
Why did you stop hugging me
I don't want any other man
I don't want any other life
I want you
Please show up at our door
And love me

Conscious Toxicity
Daria Hsu

I can't believe I just spent a night without you
under the same roof as me
We almost never spent nights in the same bed
But now it's not even under the same roof
How can you have left our children so easily
You gave Zen a hug and a kiss and talked to him
briefly
A brief kiss for Gaia sleeping in my arms
I put your bag of clothes out the door
I knew it's not good to keep having fights in which
you kept threatening to leave
You would tell me you were staying only for the
kids
In our car on the way to San Diego, I thought I
could feel your deep love for me
Yet I noticed at the safari when D and K would
briefly hug or hold hands
We stood next to each other like two awkward
rocks
And at the family dinner when A and J A would
talk to each other so light-heartedly
We didn't even look at each other and barely
uttered a word, and that only about caring for our
kids
Are you ok
Are you safe

Conscious Toxicity
Daria Hsu

You left with your bag of clothes
Without a car
In one hour it will be 24 hours since you left us
I opened the door this morning hoping the sound outside was you returning
I walked into your bedroom last night hoping you were inside
I cannot live without you
Don't you understand
How can you live without me and our children
I don't understand
Why did you ever stop hugging me
Why did you ever start pushing away every single hug
Why can't I call you honey any more
Please tell me how to go on
How to put one foot in front of the other
If the love of my life has left[1]

---

[1] I wrote this poem when Michael moved out of our apartment in Long Beach (back to his parents' house in Rowland Heights) for one night during a particularly rough patch in our marriage after sweet little baby Gaia was born, leaving me, Zen and Gaia behind. In fact, he moved out twice during that first year of Gaia's life (for one night

Conscious Toxicity
Daria Hsu

each time), and also, in response to him moving out, I took our kids to sleep in a motel room for one night as well after one of our arguments (not sure any more if I did it once or twice). It was as painful and traumatizing as it sounds. Thanks to God's grace, we were able to find back to each other.

104.

If only you knew how deeply ashamed I feel of my thoughts
Clearly something is very wrong with me
No one normal thinks like that
What kind of children am I raising with these thoughts
We are searching for a house for our family to live in
Which should be a joyful occasion
And it is
Until I find out that the previous owners were an elderly couple
Who passed away after living in the house for forty years

Conscious Toxicity
Daria Hsu

Their gorgeous house is filled with things from
their life
But I am afraid the house will be haunted by night
And I can't move in
Yet I was not scared to take free art books from
their book collection
That the realtor pointed out were up for grabs
Later I started spiraling:
If people died in the second house and I don't want
to move there
Then in the first house we visited,
Where the owner told me she was moving closer to
her son,
Did her husband die or did she get divorced?
And if I move into her house, will Michael die
Or will we get divorced?
I remember standing in one of the newly
remodeled bedrooms in that house
Feeling depressed and lonely
I am so ashamed of my thoughts
I couldn't utter them fully to my best friend
yesterday
But I live with them
They incapacitate and handicap me from a free
and joyful life
I want a million dollar mansion

Conscious Toxicity
Daria Hsu

Or maybe a cheap shack
Luxurious or simple
I don't even know where
I don't even know what I want
I want to be joyful, vibrant, healthy
But given choices I collapse
Or maybe the right choice truly hasn't come yet
Maybe I do need more time to research
And find our very own home with a backyard for the kids,
With an office space for Michael
And with peace for me.
A home free from all these incessant triggers and thoughts,
From secret painful shame of my skewed thinking where everyone is my enemy and my competitor, is envious and jealous of me, tries to manipulate me, where I'm scared of my family being demons and sociopaths out there to get me, where I'm jealous and competitive, depressed and lonely, scared and in limbo, a mother of whom kids are scared, a mother whom kids ask why are you angry, why do you cry,
A home where I can learn to be a cozy and loving, a non-scary and non-triggered mom,

Conscious Toxicity
Daria Hsu

A mom whose son doesn't say you don't need me any more
A mom who understands why her daughter is crying and uncomfortable and can soothe her
Not just hold her in silence and paralysis, unsure of what to say
A mom who doesn't spank her son (I am forever sorry Zen!)
But deals in a more appropriate manner when her three-year-old son jumps on the bed next to his sleeping baby sister and as I try to fetch him from the bed accidentally jumps on top of his sleeping sister's little body causing me to scream out in horror and anguish as I expect Gaia's guts to have burst open from the pressure, fully expecting her death
So I yell at Zen at the top of my lungs and spank his butt as hard as I can
I am supposed to take four deep breaths and walk away according to Daniel Tiger
But that is NOT what I did
Luckily Gaia was unharmed and my delusional self wonders if it was truly an accident
It was my responsibility to put her to sleep in a safe space where her brother cannot get to her

Conscious Toxicity
Daria Hsu

But in our small apartment it is hard, he is fast and strong-willed,
I failed and then blamed a three-year old
But I can't shake off this feeling that he did it on purpose
With an evil intent
But if I accuse him, make him into a criminal
When accidents happen
If he grows up with his own mother not believing in his goodness
Then who will believe in him?
The seeming rupture of our relationship after Gaia was born
The anger I take out on him
The failure to see him and treat him as a three-year old
(He makes it hard to do so, he is so smart and perceptive!!)
I have many shameful and regretful feelings and thoughts
But Gaia is my daughter and she deserves to breastfeed and co-sleep peacefully with me just like Zen did
He wants me to pick him up
But Gaia is crying on the grass
So I pick up Zen while Gaia is crying

Conscious Toxicity
Daria Hsu

And then I pick up crying Gaia and I try to hold
her as much as I can
They are my children and both deserve to be held
and breastfed and coslept with as babies
But what do toddlers, or preschoolers deserve?
My son is growing so quickly
And I don't really spend quality time with him
I have a lot of regrets
Will he remember me as a harsh, crying, angry
mother who never played with him and was
always angry at him?
Will Gaia remember me holding her and sobbing?
I wonder if my son has a mental illness
If my daughter has depression
But ironically I am the one with issues in our
family
That are not taken care of and thus absorbed by
our children
Just like I absorbed from my mother and father
And here we are, searching for a house for our
family
A home with lots of peace for me, for my sad
pained soul to heal
Yet here I am, all these years later, barely any
wiser, none the merrier

Conscious Toxicity
Daria Hsu

105.

I feel pain in my arms -
The moment we leave your parents' house,
Just as I am feeling so rested and peaceful for once
After a day of respite,
You open your foul argumentative mouth
And start an argument
You are one toxic motherfucker of a husband
I have to sit through endless, countless hours of
being told off and lectured by you
Criticizing every fucking aspect of me from my
appearance to my actions
And I sit quietly because our two kids are in the
back of our car and I know that if I speak up my
mind
You will not listen one bit
And get even more argumentative and unpleasant
and speak even louder at 11:25 PM as they are
sleeping
You are threatening me about our relationship not
being good, our marriage failing
Why don't you just shut up for once and for once
stop creating problems and arguments everywhere
and anywhere,

Conscious Toxicity
Daria Hsu

Cooking up drama out of quiet
What's the point of going to rest and sleep over at
your parents' house if the moment we leave you
are dissatisfied
I just want to sit in the car and preserve the
precious, rare feeling of rested-ness and wholeness
I was able to restore during our sleepover
But you don't let me
Immediately bring up your session with psychic N
And everything she said
You had asked me if I wanted to hear what she had
to say
I am always curious about what psychics have to
say so I said yes
But I didn't expect it to be a new barrage of
problems and complaints upon my head
You claim you want peace so why can't you live
peace?
You are accusing me of having issues as you're
driving us back to Long Beach, feeling validated by
psychic N, as I sink into my computer to type my
poem in order to disassociate from you disturbing
my equilibrium, you accuse me of bulldozing into
my computer, of staring into my screen, you are
telling me there is no point in being together and
that I may as well be single if I don't answer you,

Conscious Toxicity
Daria Hsu

you are asking me why I don't want to
communicate
What the fuck do you want me to say when I just
want to escape this disturbing interaction that is
being pushed upon me?
You and N say it's toxic that I made you drive back
up the hill to your parents' house last night to drop
off your dad before picking us up from the dollar
store
Well, I think it's toxic that your dad drove you - as
if you were a child! - to pick us up when I asked
you, my husband, to pick us up!
Why couldn't you just borrow his truck to pick up
your family, why did he drive you as if you are a
little boy? I won't have any of that! The emperor
and the empress have disempowered you enough
throughout your life as they continuously attempt
to rebuild their self-esteem and self-love by
achieving lasting financial prosperity
Our married and family life feels like a walk
through hell
I was recently told by an endocrinologist that I
have a growth in my thyroid that has a 20%
chance of developing into (or being?) cancer
This life is physically destroying me!

Conscious Toxicity
Daria Hsu

But what can I do - to leave with two children and no money in a country with barely any welfare system is a social suicide
To leave my marriage and to face my complete and utter fear of loneliness, aloneness, to abandon my youthful dream of happily ever after with you, of you being my eternal soulmate - that is a dark pit to face, the scariest part of it being the point of no return
So here I am, living in shit, in distress, growing a thyroid lump from the toxic stress of never-ending one-sided arguing on your part: always unhappy, always complaining, always overwhelmed
But also always washing the dishes (I don't remember the last time I pre-washed, loaded or unloaded the dishes from the dishwasher), always making green juice for me, always taking hours to research anti-cancer supplements for me, always cleaning up around our home, always making food for our children
I'm worried this life is killing me slowly,
But I remember that I also felt dead when you moved out
You are very caring and dedicated
There is a gaping hole without you in my life

Conscious Toxicity
Daria Hsu

But I just wish you weren't so argumentative so
often
It's killing me slowly
Sleepover at grandparents is over
Welcome back to Nebraska Ave
A home that doesn't feel like home
Ironically, the grandparents' house that I had
fought so hard to escape feels more homey and
relaxed - but maybe because it is exactly that, a
visit, where I can kick back and unapologetically
relax while grandma sweeps up the messes and
makes butter toasts for the kids all day long at our
beck and call?
Or maybe the grandparents know a secret that
we're missing to a peaceful, joyful home?
Will we ever find a home - and a state of mind -
that feels like home?

106.

I woke up
You were not in the bedroom
I knew you had stepped out
I assumed it was because Gaia kept waking up and
crying

Conscious Toxicity
Daria Hsu

I was unable to sleep without knowing where
exactly you were
And wanted to spend a little time around you - the
little time we have before kids wake up and life
becomes hectic again, turning us into roommates
under the same roof -
I quietly exited the bedroom, leaving Zen and Gaia
sleeping on the mattress
I looked in your office and in the living room but
you weren't there
I looked again, just to double check
Nope, not there
Not in the kitchen either
Our apartment is tiny so it's not easy to overlook a
person
In my rising grief and panic,
I opened the apartment door
Your shoes were gone
My immediate thought was that you were so upset
at me for writing a nasty poem about you last night
that you went for a walk but my deeper fear was
that you had had enough of this life and went
somewhere to end it all,
After all, you have often expressed lately that you
can no longer take it or something along those
lines

Conscious Toxicity
Daria Hsu

In my grief, I stormed down two flights of stairs to the garage hoping, begging to find you on this gray Long Beach morning
I opened the door into the garage and - there you were, cleaning out the car, looking for the van keys you lost
I rushed towards you, as always reprimanding you for leaving without telling me
You as always telling me that you don't need to let me know if you're just in the garage
Me as always hugging you and demanding you to hug me back
You as always letting me hug you but not hugging me back
Me as always taking your arms and trying to wrap them around my waist
You as always trying to pull back
Telling me we need counseling, bringing up psychic N being our counselor
(You told me last night that N said I hate her - I don't want to talk to someone that says that stuff, and that's in addition to her giving you advice months earlier to move out of our home, which you did, and which resolved nothing and brought us all a mountain of pain)

Conscious Toxicity
Daria Hsu

Me as always remaining quiet rather than disagreeing
Because disagreeing with you just leads to bigger, growing conflicts
And I can't afford that
I have two kids sleeping in the bedroom upstairs
And so I make sure to turn around and head for the garage door to go back up as tears begin streaming from my eyes,
Which I carefully hide from you,
Relieved that I found you, my love

Made in the USA
Las Vegas, NV
05 September 2023